The Creation
of Garfield

The Creation
of Garfield

Rodney McCance

WHITE OWL
AN IMPRINT OF PEN & SWORD BOOKS LTD.
YORKSHIRE – PHILADELPHIA

First published in Great Britain in 2021 by
White Owl
An imprint of
Pen & Sword Books Ltd
Yorkshire – Philadelphia

ISBN 978 1 52676 834 6

A CIP catalogue record for this book is
available from the British Library.

Printed and bound in the UK by CPI Group (UK) Ltd,
Croydon, CR0 4YY

Pen & Sword Books Limited incorporates the imprints of Atlas,
Archaeology, Aviation, Discovery, Family History, Fiction, History,
Maritime, Military, Military Classics, Politics, Select, Transport,
True Crime, Air World, Frontline Publishing, Leo Cooper, Remember
When, Seaforth Publishing, The Praetorian Press, Wharncliffe
Local History, Wharncliffe Transport, Wharncliffe True Crime
and White Owl.

For a complete list of Pen & Sword titles please contact

PEN & SWORD BOOKS LIMITED
47 Church Street, Barnsley, South Yorkshire, S70 2AS, England
E-mail: enquiries@pen-and-sword.co.uk
Website: www.pen-and-sword.co.uk

Or

PEN AND SWORD BOOKS
1950 Lawrence Rd, Havertown, PA 19083, USA
E-mail: Uspen-and-sword@casematepublishers.com
Website: www.penandswordbooks.com

Contents

Chapter 1

Introduction

Everyone knows Garfield the cat. He is one of the most recognizable figures of the twentieth century: his face has adorned newspaper strips, billboards, animated TV shows, movies and every other single piece of merchandise you can think of, from colouring books to lunchboxes, cat food bowls, bumper stickers and toys of every variety. Garfield is a global phenomenon. The sarcastic orange cat inspires people to hate Monday a little more, to be that little bit lazier and to indulge in their love of lasagne.

From humble small-town beginnings in rural Indiana, Garfield the cat – the creation of cartoonist Jim Davis – has become a worldwide presence since his debut in the late 1970s. He is one of the most loved and enduring comic strip characters in history, alongside Peanuts, Dilbert, Calvin and Hobbes and many more. He is even recognized by the *Guinness Book of World Records* as the most popular comic book strip in the world, syndicated in over 2,000 newspapers globally. The cat's large eyes, even larger belly and scathing sarcasm have become a staple of pop culture, relatable to many, many people over different decades and generations.

Much has been said of Davis' commercial aspirations when he first created the adorable ginger cartoon cat, and about Garfield's true authenticity. Davis has even been quoted as saying that he created the comic strip with 'a conscious effort to come up with a good, marketable character', as he told Walter Shapiro in an interview for the *Washington Post* in 1982. 'And primarily an animal ... Snoopy is very popular in licensing. Charlie Brown is not.' However, there is more to be said than that. Garfield is the meeting point between commercialization and creativity. Nobody levels the same criticisms at Walt Disney and Mickey Mouse, that the world's most famous mouse is a cynical creation, so why do so with Garfield? Garfield probably has just as much merchandise as Disney – perhaps even more – but just because the cat has been licensed many times over, does that make the character somewhat empty in many people's eyes? Does that mean that there is a lack of legitimacy in the work? It is a trait that always follows Garfield around; much like with Odie, Garfield cannot get rid of it.

The cat has permeated into the American psyche. From becoming part of the zeitgeist in the 1980s with plush toy hangars found on every car, to reinventing himself to suit the meme culture of the 2000s, Garfield's adaptability is second-to-none. His power to survive has seen him through over forty years in the mainstream, and he is still going strong. Everyone knows Garfield: he is as recognizable a brand as McDonald's, Coca-Cola or Wendy's. Whether the comic strip is on a par with creations like Calvin and Hobbes or Peanuts is questionable to some, but in terms of sheer recognizability and longevity, Davis created a marketing and cultural icon, a combination of several key elements that connected with society. Garfield has appeared in newspapers for over forty years, on best-selling book lists and even comic books. His domination of all genres of the comic strip is unmatched by any character. His reach has extended into children's animation and children's education. The intention of Garfield was to create an apolitical comic strip, something so far removed from the news that surrounded it in the newspaper. The opposite of a *New Yorker* cartoon, the joy of Garfield is that anyone can appreciate it; the strip is designed meticulously for that purpose. The craftsmanship and effort that goes into producing Garfield can sometimes be overlooked. From a young child to an elderly person, Garfield can get a laugh out of anyone; the character is evergreen. He is unrepentant in what he is, and it's this attitude that has endeared him to fans, regular readers and even people who just scan the strip in passing while perusing the newspaper. If you see a Garfield comic strip, you know what you are going to get. The same can be said of creator Jim Davis and his company Paws Inc., who created Garfield; they are unrepentant in what they wish Garfield to be. All Garfield does is insult Jon, hate Mondays and working, then criticize Odie and eat a lot of lasagne or any other available food. It doesn't get much simpler than that, which is why people adore him. The beauty is in the character's simplicity. It's a timeless comic strip that has no real defining place or time to it, so much so that Davis made a conscientious decision not to name the location where Garfield lives, wanting it to feel like Garfield could live next door to you.

'My strip Garfield really doesn't deal with any social or political comment whatsoever, that's for the rest of the paper, that's for the news broadcasts,' Davis says, ruminating on Garfield's position in the world. Given his laid-back attitude, Davis would rather bring joy to the world than offer up any political comment. It is an interesting attitude – indeed one which has been criticized – but Davis has always stuck to his guns in that regard.

So why has the popularity of this lazy, sarcastic cat prevailed since he was created in the late 1970s? What makes a lethargic orange tabby cat so enduring and endearing to the world? As well as being in the *Guinness Book of World Records*, he has – at the time of writing – over 16 million followers on Facebook and 146,000 followers on Twitter. Garfield also heads up the campaign for Safe and Secure Online, a campaign which aims to make children safe with online browsing, and in China, Garfield was for a time used as a mascot to help children learn English. With Garfield, Davis and Paws Inc. try to use the character as a learning aid to make a difference in the world. One of the biggest examples of that is Davis' non-profit collaboration with his *alma mater*, Ball State University, to create professorgarfield.org, an 'edutainment' (education and entertainment) website dedicated to providing kids struggling with dyslexia and their teachers a fun learning aid to help battle illiteracy. Professor Garfield would become the face of different cartoons, apps and games to actively help children of different needs learn to read. He also has his own national day! Celebrated each 19 June, the anniversary of the publication of his first comic strip, the day is set aside to honour all things related to the ginger feline. So Garfield works harder than many think; certainly harder than he wants you to think!

National Garfield the Cat Day was first celebrated in 1998 on the twentieth anniversary of the comic strip and Garfield's birthday. Boca Raton City Council member Wanda Thayer proclaimed 19 June as Garfield the Cat Day during a surprise birthday party at the International Museum of Cartoon Art in Boca Raton, Florida. Having a national day of celebration is no mean feat, but what would Garfield's reaction to that be? Jim Davis says:

'Garfield is an international character. Therefore, I don't even use seasons. The only holiday I recognize is Christmas. I don't use rhyming gags, plays on words, colloquialisms, in an effort to make Garfield apply to virtually any society where he may appear ... I would like for readers in Sydney, Australia to think that Garfield lives next door. Dealing with eating and sleeping, being a cat, Garfield is very universal. By virtue of being a cat, he's not really male or female or any particular race or nationality, young or old.'

For this author, his journey with reading as a whole – and his love of comic books in particular – started by collecting Garfield books. It was really my first foray into reading and into comic books. I used to take several of the books on long car journeys with my parents to keep me occupied as we travelled from Belfast to Omagh to visit family. I used to adore the pocket-sized books that were printed vertically. And I most definitely had a Garfield plush toy too.

Chapter 2

Jim Davis

Davis was born in 1945, on an 120-acre farm 5 miles outside Fairmount, Indiana. Davis describes his early years as 'one of those glorious childhoods, filled with sunshine and running through the fields, cats and dogs and animals and good times'. In postwar Indiana at the time, people found work either on farms or in the state's burgeoning automotive industry. Davis grew up with lots of cats, dogs and other animals. However, he suffered from severe asthma and, in his own words, was 'allergic to pretty much everything'. Spending a lot of time indoors, his mother encouraged him to draw when he could not go outside to play or to do chores.

Davis attended Fairmount High School (as did film star James Dean), playing in the high school football team for four years, despite his asthma. He was also in school plays for four years:

'I learned a lot about doing a comic strip, from doing theatre, because there is not much difference in it. By virtue of being the cartoonist, I get to write the script, I get to set the stage, I get to determine the blocking, determine how everybody moves and acts from that. You know, all I do is freeze frame and draw them at three frames.'

Growing up, Davis was a big fan of comic books: 'I was a big fan of Peanuts and Beetle Bailey, Hi and Lois, eventually B.C. and Wizard of Oz and also Pogo. That one, I never understood it but I'd love looking at the pictures, the artwork by Walt Kelly.'

Davis went on to Ball State Teacher's College in 1963, where he studied art education. All the while, in the back of his mind he wanted to be a cartoonist. When he was faced with having to teach art, which he didn't want to do, he switched over to business, thereby setting himself up with an education and knowledge that he would later put to good use.

He explains his thinking behind coming up with a cartoon cat:

'Garfield is based on the people I knew, rather than the animals; I just put a human personality in a cat's body. I went to a Holiday Inn in Indianapolis and just sat in a room for three days, with piles of paper and pens and thought about it. There's some truth to it that dogs are dogs. You know what your dog is thinking. Cats, they are a little withdrawn, subdued, so people tend to lend human thoughts and feelings more to cats than they do dogs, so as a result I can get away with Garfield thinking human thoughts.'

While Garfield is known for being a lazy, bored cat, his creator is the furthest thing from it. Davis' work ethic is the thing that took his comic strip from the newspapers and into every piece of merchandise than can possibly be produced. Davis' eye for an opportunity and background in marketing made him the ideal person to form a character perfect for the general public; a public eager to identify with a lazy, work-hating cat.

Times had changed when Davis created Garfield. The children of the 1950s boomers had grown up and were having children of their own. Having to become everything they hated about their parents, they perhaps identified with a lazy cat who hated work. From a hardworking background in rural Indiana, Davis grew up on a farm with lots of animals, including at least twenty-five cats.

Davis is still very hands-on in the process, but no longer writes or draws every Garfield strip. He has an entire team at Paws Inc. to do that now:

'I see gags and I work with assistants on the strip and stuff like that. We do roughs and it all filters through me so that it has one voice. We all get together occasionally in the same room and draw and work on shapes of fingers and gestures and expressions and things like that so that if any one of us draws it, you can't tell which one did it.

'What gets me out every day is the comic strip. That's what I do best and I love it. It is so much fun to do because it is really positive just sitting and thinking of funny stuff and then trying to draw a really funny picture. Here I am a grown man, still it is so much fun.'

Regarding his fame, Davis has expressed gratitude that he doesn't have to face the public:

'Being a cartoonist, you really enjoy a lot of anonymity. [If] you take a half-dozen of the biggest cartoonists and walk them down any street, nobody would notice them. They only know their characters. So I just hide behind Garfield. The only time anyone knows the name or spots me is if I'm out on [a] book tour and I'm meant to do publicity. We don't suffer any of the kind of attention problems that I think people do on TV or in movies. It's not a big deal. I'm sitting here in the countryside of East Central Indiana, so it's pretty quiet.

'I really had no desire to move away from Indiana. Friends, family, everything was right here. By virtue of having grown up on a farm, I really wanted to get back to the country, that's where I feel normal. It's great to step out of the studio and walk through the woods, have the sky as your limitation and think great things, you know, I like working in this kind of environment.'

It's the small town feeling that gives Garfield its 'mom and pop' feel, despite it being a multi-million-dollar brand.

Talking about his relationship with other creators, Davis has said:

'While I don't see them very often, I count Dean Young (Blondie), Mort Walker (Beetle Bailey), Mike Peters (Mother Goose & Grimm), and Lynn Johnston (For Better or For Worse) as friends. I was (and still am) a huge fan of Charles Schulz's work. I think Calvin and Hobbes is one of my favourite strips of all time. Talk about imagination! The strip was a masterpiece. As for some of the newer strips, Get Fuzzy cracks me up.'

Davis, clearly still a massive fan of the medium in which he works, is always quick to champion other people's work.

He has offered the following thoughts on drawing and artistic skill: 'I've always maintained there is no such thing as art talent, but there is such a thing as skill. The skill is born from having an interest in, a love of, drawing. The more you enjoy it, the more you draw, [and] the more you draw, the better you get. It's that simple.'

Chapter 3

Gnorm Gnat

Garfield was not the only anthropomorphic cartoon creation that came from the mind of Jim Davis. Before Garfield there was Gnorm Gnat. Gnorm was an anthropomorphic gnat – a tiny flying insect. Gnats can be either biting or non-biting, and it seems like Gnorm did not have the bite to make it in the harsh world of newspaper comic strips. Gnorm was the straight man in his own comic strips, which were similar in tone and style to Garfield and featured Davis' brand of mundane, slice-of-life humour. Gnorm appeared in his own comic strip that ran in *The Pendleton Times* in Davis' home state of Indiana for five years from 1972–77. Not many of the comic strips can be found today, as not many would have been kept from a small-town newspaper in the 1970s. It is a shame that not many of the strips exist, but Gnorm lives on in his own strange infamy, like an annoying gnat that won't go away.

Davis has said that Gnorm Gnat was based on the character Walter Mitty from James Thurber's *The Secret Life of Walter Mitty*, first published in *The New Yorker*. The book was a big influence on Davis, with Mitty the mild-mannered daydreamer who imagines extraordinary situations that always seem to end badly. Like Mitty, Gnorm is the 'straight man', with all sorts of whacky situations, weird characters and absurdity surrounding him.

Like Garfield, Gnorm also had a cast of side characters: Lyman, a buck-toothed insect; Freddy the fruit fly, who only has two weeks to live; the very stupid Cecil Slug; the highly intelligent Dr Rosenwurm, who is a worm; along with the villainous Drac Webb, who tries to eat the other characters. They're not the most aesthetically pleasing bunch of characters to look at in a newspaper every day, but their misadventures lasted for five years and the consistency of drawing the strip would hone Davis' skills and push him to go on to something much bigger.

Gnorm didn't have the wit or sarcasm of Garfield, and even though the strips were well received, Gnorm would never go on to star in comic strips in national newspapers or have his own movies, but some fans – and Davis himself – remember him fondly. Gnorm was an integral part in Davis finding his voice in comics. Without this tiny acerbic insect, we might not have had the sarcastic, lasagne-eating, Monday-hating orange tabby cat.

In 1969, Davis left his job at a marketing company and began working as an assistant for Tom Ryan (known as T.K. Ryan), the creator of Tumbleweeds, a satirical comic strip about life in the Old American West. This job would prove an invaluable experience for Davis, who worked with Ryan for over eight years. Davis would do sketches and pencil drawings for the daily strips, as well as formulate story ideas and help develop the scripts and gags for Tumbleweeds. In 1972, while working on Tumbleweeds, Davis developed and released Gnorm Gnat, which debuted in *The Pendleton Times* (a small newspaper based in Pendleton, Indiana) and would stay there for five years. During this time, Davis would send the comic strip out to national newspapers, trying to get it syndicated – the goal of any strip – but each time Davis only received another rejection letter. In an interview with Garfield.com, Davis said, 'I bet I received enough rejection notices to wallpaper a cathedral.' It's this sort of wry humour that permeates all of Davis' work, especially in Garfield, and would in time help him become so successful.

Davis has stated that he liked the comedic possibilities with insects, but editors didn't necessarily agree, one telling him, 'Your art is good, your gags are great, but bugs – nobody can relate to bugs!' This was one of the deciding factors in Davis putting an end to Gnorm's adventures in *The Pendleton Times*. It was a particularly blunt criticism, but Davis appreciated the honesty; it led to the demise of Gnorm the Gnat and the birth of Garfield the Cat.

Working with Ryan on Tumbleweeds, Davis gained an insight into the creation and production of comic strips. Davis said of this time, 'I learned the discipline and skills it takes to become a syndicated cartoonist by watching Tom.' Davis worked as an assistant on Tumbleweeds for over eight years, and before that he had worked at the marketing agency after graduating from Bell State University. All these things – from Tumbleweeds to the failure of Gnorm Gnat – would lead to him developing his most famous creation. In his final appearance, Gnorm would be destroyed by a giant foot, with both Gnorm and the comic strip killed off for good. Gnorm does live on, though; his eyes are the same design as those of Garfield from 1984 onward, and of course Garfield has made some in-jokes about his predecessor in various stories through the years. The name 'Lyman' was also reused for a character that would appear in Garfield several years later. Lyman in the Garfield strip was Odie's original owner, a friend and roommate of Jon Arbuckle, designed as the only other character Jon could talk to. He was one of the original four main characters in Garfield, but he was soon phased out in the early 1980s. Gnorm's legacy, if you can call it that, is one of the most iconic and fortunate failures in comic book history, and this gnat is really only remembered for his rather tragic and unusual end, which mirrored the giant foot motif often used in the *Monty Python's Flying Circus* TV series.

Mike Peters, an editorial cartoonist and author of *Mother Goose and Grimm*, has stated: 'We can always be thankful that Jim's first strip never made it … Gnorm Gnat has gone down in cartoon folklore as a most fortunate failure. Can you imagine a bright orange gnat on every car window? A great, huge gnat for the Thanksgiving Day Parade? A big fat gnat saying, "I hate Tuesdays"?' Just like that, Gnorm the Gnat was gone, resigned to becoming a little piece of trivia in conversations about its creator, Jim Davis. While Gnorm would not be able to head up a marketing department, for the people who read the strips at the time, it gave them a laugh.

Chapter 4

The First Ever Garfield Comic Strip
& Early Years

G arfield and his owner Jon Arbuckle made their comic strip debut
on 19 June 1978 in forty-one newspapers across the United States.
In the traditional three-panel comic strip, Jon introduced himself
and his cat, Garfield, to the United States audience. In an inauspicious
debut for two characters who have since become synonymous in American
and indeed worldwide popular culture, they simply introduce themselves,
with a slight joke at the end. Davis certainly didn't start out with the
world's greatest gag! Garfield and Jon look quite different from how they
are drawn today. That first comic strip reflects the other strips of the
time, looking like Peanuts, or even the style of political cartoons. Jon and
Garfield both have exceedingly small eyes; Garfield's are almost buried
in his body. But what a body! Tiny legs and paws lie at the bottom of his
blob-like form. He truly is made to look overweight and huge in these
early comic strips, his small head tucked into a large body. He of course
is a sickly orange. Whereas he would get a radical design overhaul in the
1980s, the early Garfield is more like an actual cat than the cuddly, big-
eyed anthropomorphic character we are now used to. The two characters
have thin, sketchy black ink outlines and there is a messiness to their
designs. While the characters later became more refined, to look more
kitsch and cute, these early designs make Garfield fall in line with other
contemporary strips you'd see in the newspaper.

From the very first moment, the stakes are set. The thick inky lines
that Davis became famous for began here, along with the muted colour
scheme. The first words ever spoken in a Garfield comic strip are by
Jon, 'Hi there … I'm Jon Arbuckle. I'm a cartoonist, and this is my cat
Garfield.' Garfield then replies with, 'Hi there, I'm Garfield, I'm a cat
and this is my cartoonist Jon.' Garfield's first punchline (if you can even
call it that) thought bubble in his own strip is not surprising; it is 'Feed

Me'. The strip works on two levels, the joke being that Garfield thinks that Jon is *his* human being, showing his arrogance. However, it works on a meta-level too, as Jon is also a representation of Jim Davis, who is actually Garfield's cartoonist. 'If he were a human, he'd be despicable,' Davis said of his cat, and that is certainly the case from the very first comic strip.

This strip, and many more, can be found by searching the incredible database of Garfield strips on the Garfield.com website. It is fun to search and find the strips that were in newspapers on the day you were born, or on the days of particular world events. However, even more fun is just browsing and seeing this early version of Garfield change and transform from standing on four legs, to standing on two paws and looking more human, with bigger eyes and a more rotund belly. The years 1978–80 witnesseded the most dramatic changes, but over the years, refinement has caused the character to go from a traditional comic book strip to one that resembles a cartoon animal. Davis has referred to this transition as 'almost a Darwinian evolution'. Davis has also said:

'With the comic strip, there's no audio, no animation, plus you have to freeze-frame the character in the perfect position with the perfect expression to get the idea across. You have about twenty-five words or less. You only have about 7 inches within which to work. You have to set up the plot, twist it, and resolve it in that space, so it's very tough. I love the challenge of using the economy of not only words, but of line, to get the point across.'

And that comes across with any strip from the late 1970s to the present day. While the characters may look slightly different, the aim and purpose of the strip remains the same.

Early Years

Davis says of the early days of Garfield:

'The first two or three years I got all the obvious cat gags out of the way. Now I can take advantage of the fact people know him, the familiarity is much higher. You always expected to see Snoopy lying on the doghouse, for Charlie Brown to miss the football. There are certain things that make you feel warm and fuzzy, that have happened that way all your life, like telling an old joke over again. For some of us, it just gets funnier.'

Broadway musical *Hamilton* creator Lin-Manuel Miranda describes Garfield as 'such a mix of verbal and visual humour – he can make you laugh with a patented Garfield one-liner, or a pie in the face from an unexpected location ... [he is] an ironic, detached cat who is mean to everyone and somehow all the more lovable for it'.

After a few months, Garfield was dropped by the *Chicago Sun Times*. Davis feared that was the beginning of the end. After three months, he thought the *Sun Times* would be the first of many to axe the orange tabby cat. 'Here I am, 90 days into my dream career, and I lose a newspaper,' Davis recalled. 'I thought, "This is it, it's downhill from here."' But the story would take a dramatic turn, as readers would end up starting a petition for the *Sun Times* to bring back the strip. They were furious there was no Garfield and insisted that they bring back the misadventures of Davis' cat. In the end, the *Chicago Sun Times* received over 1,600 complaints.

Garfield at Large

Garfield at Large: His First Book is notable for being the first ever compilation book of Garfield comic strips. Originally published in 1980 by Ballantine Books in the United States, the book collected the Garfield comic strips dated from 19 June 1978 to 22 January 1979. This book introduced the famous 'Garfield Format' to the burgeoning market that clamoured for collected stories. Prior to its publication, most comic strip compilations, like Peanuts and Heathcliff, were published as paperbacks, with the panels running down the page vertically. Obviously, this changed their complexion and shape from their horizontal newspaper strip originals. Of course, later Garfield books and reprints would use this format, but in these first books, Jim Davis had the idea to convince Ballantine, his publisher, to print the strips from left to right, as they would have appeared in the newspaper, thus creating 'The Garfield Format', with the book being shorter from top to bottom but much wider from side to side than the average paperback book at the time. Now there are countless books that follow this format. The book was #1 on the *New York Times* bestseller list for almost two years. Davis' and Garfield's success were perhaps integral to the creation of 'The Garfield Format'; By 1980, Garfield was appearing in nearly 800 newspapers and the beginnings of Davis' empire was starting to grow, so perhaps Davis himself had enough clout to convince his publisher to print the strips vertically. It's interesting to note that for all the commercialization of Garfield, this was something that Davis wasn't willing to budge on, standing his ground as an artist.

In a fun trivia note, in the film *Anchorman 2*, characters Brian, Brick and Champ (but not Ron, who comes into the scene feeling down) read this book in Ron's office. The film, which takes place in 1980, includes the book, which at the time the film is set was the only Garfield book released.

In the original first editions of *Garfield at Large*, the strips were published in black and white, including the Sunday strips, which originally appeared in colour in the Sunday newspaper format. *Garfield at Large* has since been republished in full colour in 2001 as part of the 'Garfield Classics' series and as part of a 'Fat Cat 3-Pack' (containing the first three books for a discounted price) in 1993 and 2001, the latter with its strips in full colour. The colourized editions correct an error which is present in all previous editions: the 23 July 1978 strip originally had the first panel (Garfield hopping down the stairs) printed as the fourth panel.

The Garfield Format

Before the release of *Garfield at Large*, there were of course collections of other comics, such as Peanuts with books like *I Love You, Snoopy*. These books were the A5 novel-sized paperbacks that would fit on a shelf alongside any novel, with the strips flowing vertically, not horizontally like in a newspaper. Often in the books, for the sake of fitting in the story, the actual box panels were trimmed or even cut off altogether. Or in the case of Snoopy and Peanuts – which may have more than three panels at times – they would often squash panels close together to fit into the format.

For most comics, it was impossible to collect these strips.

Davis felt like he needed to shake something up; as a fan of these comics and having read the collections himself, he felt there needed to be a change in the market. Wanting to collect the first year of Garfield, he became boldly creative. These rectangular books are horizontally oriented to match comic strip dimensions; Davis recalled inventing the format to better fit the books on store shelves. The ability to appeal to children in books stores, with larger and more colourful covers, was a big inspiration for Davis and marks his first marketing success.

The format proved to be so popular that even to this day comic book strips are still published in this size. Obviously, through the years, the format has been refined and more prestige collections have appeared, including slipcase books and hardcover collections. Books about superheroes from the 'golden age' like Dick Tracy and Flash Gordon have books in the format that Garfield trailblazed. Even Peanuts and Calvin and Hobbes have books in the same style.

'The Garfield Format' pioneered a collector's market within comic book strips and also gave other creators and publishers the opportunity to gain access into a different market. Davis was a pioneer in seizing this opportunity and captured the audience for a collectors market that was growing in the 1980s. It was the decade when both the speculative market and the collectors' market took off, but it was arguably the appeal of the books to children that made them special. The larger size made it easier for children to read. Almost all of the collected editions titles refer to Garfield's weight or his love of food. Below is a list of the titles of the books up until 2020, including the months they collect and publication date in the United States:

Garfield at Large: His First Book: 19 June 1978 – 22 January 1979 (16 September 1980)

Garfield Gains Weight: His Second Book: 23 January 1979 – 26 August 1979 (25 March 1981)

Garfield Bigger Than Life: His Third Book: 27 August 1979 – 30 March 1980 (8 September 1981)

Garfield Weighs In: His Fourth Book: 31 March 1980 – 2 November 1980 (15 March 1982)

Garfield Takes the Cake: His Fifth Book: 3 November 1980 – 7 June 1981 (16 June 1982)

Garfield Eats His Heart Out: His Sixth Book: 8 June 1981 – 10 January 1982 (12 February 1983)

Garfield Sits Around the House: His Seventh Book: 11 January 1982 – 15 August 1982 (10 March 1983)

Garfield Tips the Scales: His Eighth Book: 16 August 1982 – 20 March 1983 (12 February 1984)

Garfield Loses His Feet: His Ninth Book: 21 March 1983 – 23 October 1983 (12 September 1984)

Garfield Makes It Big: His 10th Book: 24 October 1983 – 27 May 1984 (12 February 1985)

Garfield Rolls On: His 11th Book: 28 May 1984 – 30 December 1984 (12 September 1985)

Garfield Out to Lunch: His 12th Book: 31 December 1984 – 4 August 1985 (12 February 1986)

Garfield Food for Thought: His 13th Book: 5 August 1985 – 11 March 1986 (12 February 1987)

Garfield Swallows His Pride: His 14th Book: 12 March 1986 – 12 October 1986 (12 September 1987)

Garfield Worldwide: His 15th Book: 13 October 1986 – 17 May 1987 (12 February 1988)

Garfield Rounds Out: His 16th Book: 18 May 1987 – 19 December 1987 (12 September 1988)

Garfield Chews the Fat: His 17th Book: 20 December 1987 – 24 July 1988 (18 February 1989)

Garfield Goes to Waist: His 18th Book: 25 July 1988 – 25 February 1989 (24 February 1990)

Garfield Hangs Out: His 19th Book: 26 February 1989 – 30 September 1989 (3 October 1990)

Garfield Takes Up Space: His 20th Book: 1 October 1989 – 5 May 1990 (13 February 1991)

Garfield Says a Mouthful: His 21st Book: 6 May 1990 – 4 December 1990 (24 September 1991)

Garfield by the Pound: His 22nd Book: 5 December 1990 – 7 July 1991 (25 February 1992)

Garfield Keeps His Chins Up: His 23rd Book: 8 July 1991 – 4 February 1992 (8 September 1992)

Garfield Takes His Licks: His 24th Book: 5 February 1992 – 5 September 1992 (10 February 1993)

Garfield Hits the Big Time: His 25th Book: 6 September 1992 – 10 April 1993 (24 August 1993)

Garfield Pulls His Weight: His 26th Book: 11 April 1993 – 9 November 1993 (20 September 1994)

Garfield Dishes It Out: His 27th Book: 10 November 1993 – 11 June 1994 (14 February 1995)

Garfield Life in the Fat Lane: His 28th Book: 12 June 1994 – 10 January 1995 (26 September 1995)

Garfield Tons of Fun: His 29th Book: 11 January 1995 – 12 August 1995 (13 February 1996)

Garfield Bigger and Better: His 30th Book: 13 August 1995 – 11 March 1996 (24 September 1996)

Garfield Hams it Up: His 31st Book: 12 March 1996 – 12 October 1996 (11 March 1997)

Garfield Thinks Big: His 32nd Book: 13 October 1996 – 13 May 1997 (7 October 1997)

Garfield Throws His Weight Around: His 33rd Book: 14 May 1997 – 13 December 1997 (6 October 1998)

Garfield Life to the Fullest: His 34th Book: 14 December 1997 – 14 July 1998 (22 February 1999)

Garfield Feeds the Kitty: His 35th Book: 15 July 1998 – 13 February 1999 (31 August 1999)

Garfield Hogs the Spotlight: His 36th Book: 14 February 1999 – 11 September 1999 (29 February 2000)

Garfield Beefs Up: His 37th Book: 12 September 1999 – 8 April 2000 (3 October 2000)

Garfield Gets Cookin': His 38th Book: 9 April 2000 – 4 November 2000 (2 October 2001)

Garfield Eats Crow: His 39th Book: 5 November 2000 – 2 June 2001 (1 January 2003)

Garfield: Survival of the Fattest: His 40th Book: 3 June 2001 – 29 December 2001 (3 February 2004)

Garfield Older and Wider: His 41st Book: 30 December 2001 – 27 July 2002 (25 January 2005)

Garfield Pigs Out: His 42nd Book: 28 July 2002 – 22 February 2003 (7 February 2006)

Garfield Blots Out the Sun: His 43rd Book: 23 February 2003 – 20 September 2003 (30 January 2007)

Garfield Goes Bananas: His 44th Book: 21 September 2003 – 17 April 2004 (28 August 2007)

Garfield Large & In Charge: His 45th Book: 18 April 2004 – 13 November 2004 (29 January 2008)

Garfield Spills the Beans: His 46th Book: 14 November 2004 – 11 June 2005 (30 September 2008)

Garfield Gets His Just Desserts: His 47th Book: 12 June 2005 – 7 January 2006 (27 January 2009)

Garfield Will Eat For Food: His 48th Book: 8 January 2006 – 5 August 2006 (25 August 2009)

Garfield Weighs His Options: His 49th Book: 6 August 2006 – 3 March 2007 (26 January 2010)

Garfield Potbelly of Gold: His 50th Book: 4 March 2007 – 29 September 2007 (31 August 2010)

Garfield Shovels It In: His 51st Book: 30 September 2007 – 26 April 2008 (25 January 2011)

Garfield Lard of the Jungle: His 52nd Book: 27 April 2008 – 22 November 2008 (30 August 2011)

Garfield Brings Home The Bacon: His 53rd Book: 23 November 2008 – 20 June 2009 (31 January 2012)

Garfield Gets in a Pickle: His 54th Book: 21 June 2009 – 16 January 2010 (11 September 2012)

Garfield Sings for His Supper: His 55th Book: 17 January 2010 – 14 August 2010 (12 March 2013)

Garfield Caution: Wide Load: His 56th Book: 15 August 2010 – 12 March 2011 (10 September 2013)

Garfield Souped Up: His 57th Book: 13 March 2011 – 8 October 2011 (28 January 2014)

Garfield Goes To His Happy Place: His 58th Book: 9 October 2011 – 5 May 2012 (26 August 2014)

Garfield the Big Cheese: His 59th Book: 6 May 2012 – 1 December 2012 (27 January 2015)

Garfield Cleans His Plate: His 60th Book: 2 December 2012 – 29 June 2013 (25 August 2015)

Garfield Chickens Out: His 61st Book: 30 June 2013 – 25 January 2014 (10 May 2016)

Garfield Listens To His Gut: His 62nd Book: 26 January 2014 – 23 August 2014 (20 December 2016)

Garfield Cooks Up Trouble: His 63rd Book: 24 August 2014 – 21 March 2015 (13 June 2017)

Garfield Feeds His Face: His 64th Book: 22 March 2015 – 17 October 2015 (12 December 2017)

Garfield Eats and Runs: His 65th Book: 18 October 2015 – 14 May 2016 (15 May 2018)

Garfield Nutty as a Fruitcake: His 66th Book: 15 May 2016 – 10 December 2016 (11 December 2018)

Garfield Slurps and Burps: His 67th Book: 11 December 2016 – 8 July 2017 (11 June 2019)

Garfield Belly Laughs: His 68th Book: 9 July 2017 – 3 February 2018 (17 December 2019)

It looks unlikely that they'll ever run out of puns for these books!

Chapter 5

The Featured Characters

Garfield

As we have seen, on 19 June 1978, Garfield was released to the world in over forty newspapers across America. The strip is quite simple and in line with those like Peanuts: it has three panels and usually a sequential story, with a punchline in the last panel. Garfield is unrecognizable in this strip, lurched over like a cat and with a lot of weight and a drooping face. He is more feline in the first strip, rather than the anthropomorphic character he became.

'I did two things – consciously,' said Davis. 'When I designed Garfield and Odie, I never referenced the first cat or dog picture. Nothing about their anatomy – nothing. For a couple of years, I would create the gestures in a mirror and sketch from that. And I made the eyes big because strips were being printed smaller.'

Garfield was named after Davis' grandfather, James A. Garfield Davis, who in turn was named after US President James A. Garfield. It is hard to argue which Garfield is better known – a former President of the United States or an iconic comic strip character.

In an interview about the famous cat, Davis said, 'You can't really read [cats]. Dogs, you can read. You know what's on a dog's mind. If he wants to bite you, it's painfully obvious. Or if he's done something wrong, you know, they're terrible liars. But cats, they're pretty special when it comes to that, so I figured I could get away with it. Garfield is a human in a cat suit.'

He also said that he 'would like for readers in Sydney, Australia to think that Garfield lives next door', and that certainly comes across in the strip. Davis intentionally tries to make the strip feel like it could be set anywhere. There's no sense of time or place within the strip, only the absurdity of the situations. Another fun fact: in every country across the world bar three, Garfield is called Garfield. The only places where Garfield is not

Garfield are Sweden, Finland and Norway (but oddly not Denmark, the other Scandinavian country), where he is called Gustav! Gustav also hates Mondays and loves lasagne; in fact he is exactly the same.

Davis says:

> 'If he lost weight, that would effectively end Garfield as we know it. Garfield sends a healthy message in that he's not perfect. He knows that and he's cool with that. He's happy with himself. If everybody were, there would probably be fewer disorders of all natures. In fact, he's the imperfection in all of us underneath. I think that makes him probably easier to identify with than a slim, athletic character in the comics.
>
> 'Yeah, I love lasagna. I thought it would be funny to have a cat who likes lasagna but as it turns out, I hear from people all the time that their cats love lasagna.'

Jon

On the same day as Garfield was introduced to the world, we were also introduced to his owner, Jonathan Quentin Arbuckle. The dynamic between the two was there to see from day one. Many are unaware, but when Jim Davis first began sending the strip to publishers it was titled 'Jon' and the comic book strip was actually about Jon, instead of Garfield. Jon was intended to be the focus of the story, with Garfield as a secondary character who pointed out flaws and foibles in Jon's character. Davis told *Mental Floss* magazine:

> 'I ran some early ideas at a local paper to see how I felt about it and I called the strip "Jon". It was about him, but he had this wise cat who, every time, came back zinging him. He always had the great payoff. At the time, I worked for T.K. Ryan – the cartoonist for Tumbleweeds – and I showed it to him and told him how every time I got to the punchline the cat zings him. And T.K. said, "Well, what does that tell you, Jim? The strip must be about the cat. Go with it."'

And with that Jon became relegated to a secondary character. The 'Jon' strip ran in *The Pendelton Times* and became the precursor to Garfield, after Gnorm Gnat. Much to the benefit of the comic strip, Jon was relegated to becoming the deuteragonist of the comic strip. Jon became somewhat of a loveable loser, with a slightly depressive and clumsy personality. Based on Davis himself, he has brown hair, green eyes and usually wears a blue polo top, which has become something of a signature look. Jon is a cartoonist in the book, adding a bit of meta-appeal and signalling the fact he is definitely based on Davis himself.

'That's true,' Davis admitted. 'Snoopy actually never talked. I didn't do it because he didn't talk, but I always felt like you watch pet owners and they talk to their animals like they understand.'

Odie

Odie is Jon's dog, originally given to him by supporting character Lyman. Odie resembled a beagle, with yellow fur, long brown ears, spots on his belly and a black button nose. Like any good dog, he is usually excitable, with his massive red tongue sticking out of his mouth. Odie is portrayed as a stupid, slobbering but happy-go-lucky, kind and ultimately loveable dog. He is loyal, innocent and dim-witted. Odie is one of the only characters to not have thought balloons (though there are some exceptions), as he is portrayed as a normal dog. Garfield occasionally refers to him as 'honest, true blue, and decent', gaining a deep respect for his dog 'brother' through the years, but of course he does not let those feelings show too often. In the animated series *The Garfield Show*, Odie is the enemy of a cat called Harry, and the plots usually involve Garfield and Odie foiling Harry's schemes to eat bluebirds.

The name Odie came from a car dealership commercial written by Jim Davis, which featured Odie the Village Idiot. Davis liked the name Odie and decided to use it again. When the Garfield strip was first submitted, Davis called Odie 'Spot'. He then visited cartoonist Mort Walker to show him his strips, and Walker told Davis, 'I had a dog named Spot.' Davis asked, 'Really?' Walker replied, 'Yes, in "Boner's Ark", one of my comic strips.' Soon after hearing this, Davis changed the dog's name to Odie.

Odie first appeared in the strip on 8 August 1978, which is now considered his birthday. He was originally a pet to Jon Arbuckle's roommate, Lyman, but Lyman disappeared from the series after about five years. He once had dialogue, on 15 June 1980 saying 'I'm hungry', which sounds like something Garfield would say! He can also be seen laughing at Garfield in the 13 January 1979 strip.

Odie is often kicked or pushed off the table by Garfield, or is the victim of some practical joke. Odie usually has a long, stretchy tongue and slobbers. In 2000, he was seen walking on two feet, instead of all fours, just like Garfield.

Odie is often the butt of Garfield's jokes, and is subject to a range of tortures and torments from the orange tabby cat, but he never gets tired of it and still seems to love Garfield.

In the live-action films, Odie is played by dachshunds Tyler and Chloe.

Pooky

Pooky is Garfield's small teddy bear and best friend. Pooky debuted on 23 October 1978, when Garfield discovered him in a drawer. His most recent appearance at the time of compiling this book was 2 February 2020, meaning they've been together for 42 years.

Pooky is a brown bear with two button eyes, a large black nose, pink paw pads and pink inner ears. In earlier comics, he appeared completely brown. Pooky has been the subject of many episodes of Garfield.

Garfield's relationship with Pooky is an interesting one. In some strips, Garfield talks to him as if he were a living animal. He can also be protective of Pooky: when Pooky lost an eye, Garfield requested a new one for him as his Christmas present. Garfield is very affectionate towards Pooky, often grabbing him in hugs, which bizarrely makes Jon Arbuckle jealous, as Jon does not get the same affection from Garfield. What does he expect; he is a cat! Pooky is generally portrayed as sentient and aware, but ultimately immobile. In a certain strip, Pooky rollerblades past Jon, who assumes Garfield is playing a prank. However, we then see Garfield at the other end of the room, implying that Pooky is skating under his own power. Pooky is also often seen in peril and has had plenty of close calls, such as losing a leg, an arm and that eye, but Garfield has always been by his side, more or less ...

Pooky is Garfield's closest confidante. In a 1987 strip when Garfield has amnesia, Pooky cries out a tear when Garfield does not want to play with him – Jon and Odie also cry. Can a cat even have amnesia? Pooky has an absent mind himself, but has no brain or common sense, because he is a teddy bear. Pooky is seen as sentient in some sequences, for example being seen as a large bear with Garfield on his lap. He enjoys what Garfield does because Pooky is his only friend who does not criticize his sloppy attitude. He is the sidekick of the 'Caped Avenger', also wearing a cape. Pooky cameos in *Garfield: The Movie* and *Garfield: A Tail of Two Kitties*. Pooky is considerably bigger in the first film, and is more in line with the plush style toy he is in the comic book strip. In the sequel he is a tiny Ty-Beanie Baby doll that has a rattle inside of him. In *The Garfield Show*, Nermal the kitten steals Pooky from Garfield to blackmail him to be nice to him, while in another episode, Pooky is kidnapped by the next-door neighbour's cat, Hercules. In one of the strips, Garfield is watching television with Pooky and leaves Pooky on the couch. When Jon walks by, the TV programme has changed to a nature documentary about bears.

Some trivia for Pooky is that Garfield is the one who gave Pooky his name, not Jon. In the very first comic strip that Pooky appears in, Garfield actually insults the poor teddy bear, calling it 'dumb, stupid, and silly-looking'. Some fans believe that Pooky originally appears in a 1977 edition of the Jon comic book. Jon is seen offering Garfield some cat food; Garfield, who is wrapped up under his blanket with just his eyes poking out, then holds out a teddy bear. While the bear is unnamed, it sure does look like Pooky!

Dr Liz

Dr Elizabeth 'Liz' Wilson – who first appeared in the strip on 26 June 1979 – is one of the main secondary characters of the Garfield franchise. She is Garfield's vet and Jon Arbuckle's love interest.

In the comic, Jon attempted to ask Liz out on a date many times over the years, but rarely succeeded. When she did accept, the outings were usually disastrous (commonly because of Garfield coming on the date or Jon doing something embarrassing).

In 2006, whilst on a date with an amnesiac called Ellen, Jon discovers that Liz is at the same restaurant dating someone else. After an awkward encounter with each other, Liz finally admits that she has feelings for Jon. The two have been portrayed as a couple since then, though Jon's trademark geekiness continues to both amuse and embarrass Liz.

Her first television appearance was on the second TV special, 'Garfield on the Town'. In all animated media she is voiced by Julie Payne, while in the live-action films she is portrayed by Jennifer Love Hewitt. In the films, she becomes Jon's girlfriend and later accepts his proposal of marriage. However, this is not mentioned in or connected to the strips.

Julie Payne is perhaps most famous for a role later in life as Larry David's mother-in-law in *Curb Your Enthusiasm*.

Dr Liz is a veterinarian, and of course is the vet of Garfield. She can be sarcastic and smart-mouthed, but is also sweet, kind, caring and animal-loving.

Although she has somewhat of a deadpan and sardonic persona, Liz rarely reacts negatively to Jon's outlandish, goofball behaviour, even finding it endearing enough on one occasion to give him a date. After becoming his full-time girlfriend, Liz continues to maintain her stoic personality, but balances this with her best attempts to be supportive of Jon.

Originally, Liz treated Garfield as a simple patient and did not show much of an interest in him. When she became Jon's girlfriend, Liz attempted to make peace with Garfield, but he was initially jealous of her as he felt that she was moving in on their lifestyle, as well as being a vet who gave him grief about his weight! Garfield eventually became happy with her presence, and now tolerates Liz at a bare minimum, much like Jon. Indeed, Garfield generally merely tolerates humans.

Nermal

Nermal is known as Garfield's main and direct nemesis in the Garfield franchise. He first appeared in the comic strip on 3 September 1979, and his latest appearance (at the time of writing) was on 29 February 2020. He has also appeared in the television programmes *Garfield and Friends* and *The Garfield Show*, as well as in the straight-to-DVD movies *Garfield Gets Real*, *Garfield's Fun Fest* and *Garfield's Pet Force*. He also made an appearance in *Garfield: The Movie*, although he looked completely different from the kitten in the comic strip.

Nermal's gender has been a subject of debate with fans of Garfield for a while. Some have mistaken Nermal for a female kitten because of his eyelashes, his seemingly feminine personality and the feminine-sounding tone of his voice in the *Garfield and Friends* cartoon. I guess it's easy to be confused. Jim Davis often gives younger characters eyelashes, including Garfield himself in the 'Garfield' segment of 'Garfield: His 9 Lives' and Orson at the beginning of the 'U.S. Acres' comic strip.

In *Garfield and Friends*, Nermal's voice was provided by Desirée Goyette. From *Garfield Gets Real* onwards, he is voiced by Jason Marsden, thereby breaking the gender confusion. He was voiced by David Eigenberg in *Garfield: The Movie*.

The Latin American dub of *Garfield and Friends* had Nermal renamed 'Telma', and his gender changed to female. After season one, 'Telma' was changed back to Nermal. Despite this, Nermal's gender only changed back to male near the end of the series.

Nermal is a cute grey tabby cat whom Garfield is jealous of. Although he can be nice on occasion, Nermal regularly and often intentionally annoys Garfield, which usually results in Garfield trying to ship him to Abu Dhabi. Nermal often comes in unannounced (and usually on Garfield's birthday), much to Garfield's dismay. Nermal acts as a smart aleck towards Garfield (much like Arlene, Garfield's occasional girlfriend). There also are times where Nermal seems to be almost as arrogant as Garfield, possibly even more so.

When he first appeared, it was stated that Nermal was owned by Jon's parents, which was never mentioned again (nor is he seen on Jon's parents' farm). When he appears, it is usually because Jon must babysit him.

Nermal shares a few physical features with Garfield. He revels in his cuteness, proudly proclaiming himself the cutest kitten in the world. Nermal can also be quite devious at times, such as when he tricked Garfield into thinking there was a shark in his water bowl by swimming in it with a shark fin. Nermal takes great pleasure in irritating Garfield, in spite of Garfield being bigger and stronger than him (Garfield tells the audience that Nermal might not live to see his next birthday on one such occasion). However, Nermal is shown to secretly look up to Garfield and sees him as his best friend, despite Garfield mistreating him.

In *The Garfield Show*, Nermal often acts smugly towards Garfield, and sometimes blackmails him into being nice to him or playing with him, possibly due to years of Garfield being mean to him. Nermal is also much more arrogant than in previous incarnations.

Arlene

Arlene made her first appearance on 17 December 1980, and her name was first mentioned a day later. The character was regularly featured in the 1980s, but has been featured less frequently since then, mostly making appearances in the cartoons and *The Garfield Show*. Arlene was also supposed to appear in what was meant to be Garfield's first animated feature film, *Garfield's Judgement Day*, which was cancelled due to Davis being unable to find a financial backer. In *Judgement Day*, it was established that Arlene is a stray cat.

Arlene is a tall, slim, long-tailed cat with pink fur, with a long and narrow neck and big red lips. Try to find a cat like her in the real world! Like Garfield and many other characters, her appearance changes through the years. Earlier in the strip's run, she has a gap between her two front teeth, which Garfield makes the subject of comedy. In the comic strips, she has three fingers (including her thumb) like Odie. In the straight-to-video movies and *The Garfield Show*, she actually has four fingers on her paws.

Arlene is Garfield's on-off girlfriend who regularly and successfully cracks jokes at the expense of Garfield. She loves to make smart remarks about him, most likely regarding his enormous ego. Garfield likewise makes fun of Arlene's teeth, sometimes resulting in physical revenge on him. They have quite a curious relationship.

Arlene is often portrayed as being deeply interested in furthering her relationship with Garfield, which is somewhat complicated by Garfield's love of food and himself. Garfield regularly tries to get her dinner from a trash can, and their relationship can be fractious, though they share a love for fish and doughnuts.

Binky the Clown

Binky the Clown is a TV personality in the world of Garfield, known for screaming catchphrases like 'Hey kids' and his obnoxious and annoying personality. Binky seeped into the Garfield comics in the 1980s as a very minor character and would make sporadic appearances thereafter, mostly on the television programmes that Garfield watches or even posters on the street. Binky the Clown makes his first appearance in *Garfield's*

Halloween Adventure, when the character was given a voice. The clown's first comic appearance was on 15 September 1986, when he was shown in an advertisement for the circus. The very next day, Garfield signs up to the circus and comes out dressed like a clown, then on 17 September, Binky gets to meet Garfield. The next day, Garfield slaps Binky with a paddle and an immense hatred between the two is born.

Binky resembles a typical clown, appearing in the Garfield comic strips and television shows dressed in a green polka-dot costume, with pink dots and a high collar, which is supplemented by a green and blue cone hat and a blue tutu. He wears white facial makeup, has messy red hair and his eyes are yellow. Binky is thought to be a send-up of Bozo the Clown, who is perhaps the most famous clown in the USA, though not so much in other countries. The character of Bozo was created by Alan W. Livingston and portrayed by Pinto Colvig for a children's storytelling recording and illustrated read-along book set in 1946. He became popular and served as the mascot for Capitol Records.

The character first appeared on US television in 1949, played by Colvig. After the creative rights to Bozo were purchased by Larry Harmon in 1956, the character became a common franchise across the United States, with local television stations producing their own Bozo shows featuring the character.

It is in *Garfield and Friends* where Binky starts to become much more prominent. The annoying clown features heavily in several episodes and has a new catchphrase, 'hey, cat'.

'Screaming with Binky' was one of the short feature segments within *Garfield and Friends*. Each segment would focus on Binky using his typically loud greeting, which would have devastating effects on the scene; the result would usually damage or destroy structures and/or cause a person to mess up a procedure. These segments aired during the second and third season of *Garfield and Friends*.

Binky and Garfield often break the 'fourth wall', talking to the audience or delivering in-jokes about the episodes. This is highlighted in 'The Feline Philosopher', an episode of *Garfield and Friends* where Binky reappears after not being featured in the series for several episodes.

Chapter 6

From Newspapers to Bookstores

The success of Garfield is hard to pin down. The transition from newspaper gags to collections and compendiums of the best strips in books, being sold in bookshops, school fairs and drug stores across the country, was certainly a stroke of marketing genius that helped to pave the way for the rest of the Garfield merchandise. It even laid the foundations for other comic strips that saw the trajectory and marketing power of Garfield and wanted in on the action. Garfield was a recognizable face in newspapers, but there were a multitude of children and adults who did not read the newspapers. Garfield's first book, titled *Garfield's First Book*, hit the *New York Times* bestseller list, debuting at #1. It was in the magic of the books where the Garfield character really took off and the strength of Davis' marketing power was truly felt.

Ballantine Books

Ballantine Books, a publisher based in New York City, was founded in 1953 by Ian and Betty Ballantine. It was acquired by Random House in 1973, and Random House would in turn be bought out by Bertelsmann in 1998.

Since 1980, Ballantine Books has published numerous Garfield books, primarily compilations of the comic strip, but it has also published special collections and other material. Garfield has featured in all kinds of books, most notably special anniversary editions such as *20 Years And Still Kicking: Garfield's 20th Anniversary Collection* and *30 Years of Laughs & Lasagna: The Life & Times of a Fat, Furry Legend!* Garfield has also had numerous holiday specials, trivia books and special one-off editions like *Garfield's Judgement Day*.

The book collections, which are usually released twice a year by Ballantine Books, contain reprints of the comic strip as it appears in daily newspapers. These books were originally printed in black and white, but from Volume 37 have been in full colour. Each book collects approximately six months of comic strips, including the Sunday strips. The Garfield comic strips are reprinted much the same in the compilation books, but the added value of reading the strips together adds layers to the story.

Garfield at Large was the first Garfield comic strip compilation book, featuring comics from 19 June 1978 to 22 January 1979. It was first published on 16 September 1980. A larger, coloured version was published in 2001. The blurb on the back of this book sums it up:

> 'Like every great lasagna, Garfield was born in the kitchen of an Italian restaurant on a winter's night in 1978, while outside snow fell like grated Parmesan cheese. He weighed five pounds, six ounces at birth – that's big for a kitten! – and right from the start showed a passion for Italian food. The restaurant owner, forced to choose between Garfield and closing his doors for lack of pasta, sold Garfield to a pet store. Garfield thought he was a goner until Jon Arbuckle walked in the door.
>
> 'The rest is history.'

Early designs of the characters were cruder, more resembling comic strips that might feature in *The Far Side* or *Raw Magazine* than the cute characters that they would become.

Notable Strips and Storylines

Halloween 1989

Davis said in an interview in the *Edmonton Journal* (https://edmontonjournal.com/entertainment/celebrity/garfields-jim-davis-talks-lasagna-bill-murray-and-40-years-of-earths-most-famous-cat):

> 'It was Halloween, I wanted to do something scary. I researched it: everyone's greatest fear is being alone. What it turned out doing is creeping out the licensees and syndicate. [Laughs] "This is not a direction, is it, Jim? Are we getting cerebral here?"'

While Garfield already had a 'Halloween Adventure' in the form of the special broadcast on Halloween 1985, it was in October 1989 that fans of the cat would get a true shock. Beginning on Monday 23 October, Garfield slowly realises he is alone, with no sign of Jon or Odie. Plastered over the scene is not a thought bubble but a purple strip with black text, with the words 'You Have No Idea How Alone You Are, Garfield'. The story then enters very bizarre territory, Garfield finding that his home has been abandoned for years, meaning he hasn't lived there for years.

Davis has explained the reason for Garfield's often surreal Halloween storylines:

'During a writing session for Halloween, I got the idea for this decidedly different series of strips. I wanted to scare people. And what do people fear most? Why, being alone. We carried out the concept to its logical conclusion and got a lot of responses from readers. Reaction ranged from "Right on!" to "This isn't a trend, is it?"'

Garfield has always seemed to thrive in the 'gag-a-day' format, often with similar themes running through all the strips that appear in a single week. In recent years, Garfield strips for the days preceding and following Halloween have typically shown our feline hero passing comment on horror movies that he watches on TV. But storylines which spanned a week, or several weeks, were more common in the earlier years of the strip's run.

The six stories which were first published in the week leading up to Halloween 1989 are unlike any other Garfield comic strips, because they are not supposed to be funny. That's right, for six days, Jim Davis' ethos for the Garfield strip went out of the window. Instead, they are intended to be frightening. This one tells the story of Garfield suddenly finding himself in a future in which Jon and Odie no longer exist. The cat is left completely on his own, and without any food, in a house which has long been abandoned.

This was a massive step away from what Garfield had been before, a radical departure for a series that was just a 'joke-a-day' strip. Davis attempted to do something more.

Waking up, Garfield feels that the house is strangely cold. He comments that he feels 'an eerie sensation' and then starts to think, 'This doesn't feel like home.' Garfield soon finds that there is nobody else in the house. He tries to reassure himself that the house is only temporarily empty, and that maybe he's dreaming. In the second panel of the third strip in the series, he thinks, 'Jon must be at the grocery store.' The final panel of the third strip shows the exterior of Garfield's house. Seeing an old 'For Sale' sign in front of the house, Garfield panics. Upon going outside, he finds that the windows and the front door have been boarded up, and the front garden is overgrown. It is obvious that the house has been abandoned for a long time.

The fourth strip in the series introduces the possibility that Garfield may now be a ghost who is haunting his former home. Having come to the realization that nobody has lived in the old house for many years, Garfield concludes that he cannot have lived there for many years either. Nevertheless, it is his house. In response to a noise and a light, Garfield runs into the kitchen. Jon and Odie are there. Jon greets Garfield and offers him a bowl of cat food. However, the food, Jon and Odie suddenly disappear. They were merely hallucinations. A caption at the end of the fifth strip in the series says that Garfield is 'locked fast within a time when he no longer exists'.

A caption at the start of the sixth strip in the series says that the only way that Garfield can overcome this terrible situation is through denial. It is rare for the Garfield comic strips to have these insert captions, as it is usually Garfield who breaks the fourth wall; these are more like something out of a superhero strip such as Superman. Down and broken, Garfield thinks, 'I don't want to be alone.' Jon and Odie then reappear, with Jon again offering Garfield some food. Foregoing the food, Garfield hugs the much-surprised Jon.

The storyline ends on a rather ambiguous note. A caption in the final panel of the sixth strip speaks of the power of imagination. It says that imagination can alter your perception of the past and present, and can also 'paint a future so vivid that it can entice … or terrify'. This can be understood as meaning that Garfield merely imagined that he was in a terrifying future and has now returned to the present reality. What was intended to be reality and what was intended to be fantasy in these six comic strips is, however, not made explicitly clear. For Davis to write something so challenging and poignant for his character is quite profound, especially when the Garfield comic strips had trodden such familiar ground for so many years.

This was the first time that Garfield had a continuous comic strip from day to day, rather than a 'one-and-done' strip. These Halloween stories did not have a joke or a gag, and must have been quite shocking for someone who read the paper for a Garfield comic strip. There was a creativity and confidence in these strips, and they are fondly remembered because they are different. Garfield isn't known for its creativity, it's known for doing the same thing – day in, day out – but on six days around Halloween 1989, newspaper readers got the opportunity to see Davis push the boundaries just a little bit.

Why there weren't more Garfield strips that challenged the reader and pushed the limits of creativity we will never know. Apart from things like *Garfield's Judgement Day*, Garfield the comic strip and Garfield the cartoon returned to their normal formatting and the status quo of the 'gag-a-day' strip.

Garfield's Judgement Day

Garfield's Judgement Day is a Garfield book based on an unfinished animated feature, published in 1990. Unlike the other Garfield books, this is in a picture book format rather than in the comic book format of all the others. Much like the Halloween story of 1989, *Garfield's Judgement Day* features a slightly different twist on the Garfield formula.

Garfield's Judgement Day starts with Garfield dreaming about all sorts of different junk food, before a beam of sunlight coming through the window wakes him up. Garfield and Odie wake up Jon, who starts to make them breakfast, but then kicks them out when they make a mess. Meanwhile down the street, Al and Fredo, twin dogs who live with the Rossini family, start to wake up Mr and Mrs Rossini along with their five kids. A few houses away from them, elderly Eli is woken up by his senior dog Barney. Eli shouts at Barney, but not in an angry way.

Garfield and Odie stand outside, feeling a sense of dread washing over them. All the other animals in the yards start to feel the same. Odie and Garfield become very afraid, and silently beg for Jon to let them in. Jon eventually lets them inside, but their uneasy feeling remains. They slowly begin to realise that it is Judgement Day, and the story follows the drama of Garfield, Odie, Jon and the neighbourhood pets who all have to deal with the destruction and chaos surrounding them. The book is notable as being the only Garfield book in which the Garfield characters talk to humans. The story also establishes Arlene as being a stray cat, as well as that Odie can't speak and has the mindset of an actual dog. The book also expanded upon the neighbourhood where Garfield lives, giving him new characters to interact with.

Veterans Day Controversy

Davis attracted criticism from the media for a Garfield strip that appeared in newspapers on 11 November 2010 in which the last panel appeared to be a negative reference to Veterans Day. Davis quickly apologized for the poorly timed comic strip, saying that it had been written a year in advance and that both his brother and son were veterans. While the controversy had no long-term effects on Garfield, it is a blemish on an otherwise impeccable career. It seemed like it was just an unfortunately timed incident and that Davis was well-respected enough that he could give a meaningful and heartfelt apology.

The thought bubble in the strips first panel reads, 'If you squish me, I shall become famous!' The spider continues, 'They will hold an annual day of remembrance in my honor, you fat slob,' referring to Garfield holding a paper up high, ready to squash the spider. The final panel shows the spider dangling above a teacher's desk while he addresses a group of other spiders: 'Does anyone here know why we celebrate "National Stupid Day"?'

Davis called the strip's appearance on Veterans Day 'the worst timing ever'. Unfortunately, he received a large amount of criticism from the media, with many national and international outlets picking up on the story. However, the strip wasn't cancelled, and the story simply blew over after Davis issued an apology. 'The strip that runs in today's paper seems to be making a statement about Veterans Day. It absolutely, positively has nothing to do with this important day of remembrance,' he said in a letter which he published the same day, addressed to friends, fans and veterans. 'I had no idea when writing it that it would appear today – of all days,' he continued. 'I do not use a calendar that lists holidays and other notable days, so when this strip was put in the queue, I had no idea it would run on Veterans Day.' Davis said his brother served in Vietnam, and his son has performed tours of duty in Iraq and Afghanistan. 'You'd have to go a long way to find someone who was more proud and grateful for what our veterans have done for all of us,' he added.

In the letter, Davis stated that he did not intend to make the same mistake again: 'You can bet I'll have a calendar that lists EVERYTHING by my side in the future.' It seems that Garfield and Davis were forgiven for the unfortunate gaffe, which was seen as a simple mistake and a misjudged effort.

Chapter 7

Themes

The Garfield comic strip is often seen as quite simple, and the themes within it can reflect this. Davis has mentioned his search for the perfect gag and to make every reader laugh. Many of the jokes in Garfield revolve around issues such as Garfield's obsessive eating and obesity, his dislike of spiders, his hatred of Mondays, his frequent diets, physical exertion, his need for coffee, his constant shedding of fur (which infuriates Jon) and his abuse of Odie and Jon. Garfield also has an obsession with mailing Nermal to Abu Dhabi, or simply throwing him through the front door. Though he will eat nearly anything (he is known to hate raisins and spinach), Garfield's favourite food is, of course, lasagne, but he also enjoys eating Jon's houseplants and other pets (mainly birds and fish).

Garfield has a curious relationship with household pests. He generally spares mice, despite them being a cat's mortal enemy – he even cooperates with them to cause mischief, much to Jon's chagrin – but will readily swat or pound flat spiders, which he despises.

Much of the humour in the Garfield strip, particularly in its early history, comes from the fact that it is based around Jon and his many foibles and insecurities. The jokes focus on Jon's poor social skills and inability to get dates with women, most notably Liz, whom he eventually starts dating. When he did get a date, it usually went awry; Jon's dates have slashed his tyres, been tranquilized and called the police when he stuck carrots in his ears. The storylines featuring Jon's dates rarely appear now. Whereas he previously had dates with many odd characters, he now exclusively dates Liz.

In much the same way as say a *Looney Tunes* cartoon, Garfield tells the same joke over and over, in different ways, just like Wile E. Coyote trying to catch Roadrunner.

While Garfield's world is designed to feel like it could be anywhere, it does have some specific locations that appearin the comic strips, such as the vet's office – a place he obviously hates with a passion. Irma's Diner is another setting in the strips that Jon frequents. Irma, a chirpy but slow-witted manager, is one of Jon's few friends, along with Lyman and Liz, until the latter becomes his girlfriend. In the diner, the bad food is the butt of most of the jokes, along with the poor management on display. Jon will also on occasion visit his parents and brother on the farm, which is mostly used in strips for holidays such as Christmas. This often results in week-long comical displays of stupidity by Jon and his family, but generally ends with a typical slice of Americana sweetness. Jon's mother and father in the strip are based on Davis' parents, but whether Jon's very simple brother, Doc Boy, is based on the creator's siblings isn't as clear. Doc Boy and his small-town leanings are often the subject of humour. There is a comic strip where Doc Boy is watching two socks spin in a dryer and seems to think it is entertainment. Frequently, the characters break the 'fourth wall' to explain jokes to the reader. This explores the relationship between the reader and Garfield, and it's most often used to explain something to the readers or talk about a subject that sets up the strip's punchline (like Jon claiming that pets are good for exercise just before he finds Garfield in the kitchen and chases him out). It can also be a mere glare when a character is belittled or not impressed. It is maybe another reason why Garfield has lasted so long, as the connection between Garfield and the reader seems to have only strengthened over time. As simple as the comic strip can be, Garfield always trusts the reader and plays Jon off to be the stupid one, and perhaps we get a strange pleasure out of that.

Chapter 8

Paws, Inc.

P aws, Inc. is an American comic book studio, animation studio and production company which was founded in 1981 by Jim Davis in order to facilitate the production and merchandising of Garfield. It was created to support the Garfield comic strip and its licensing, founded two years after the first publication of the Garfield strip. Originally starting with Davis and a few other employees, it has grown to become a multi-million-dollar business generating huge revenues, and was eventually sold to Nickelodeon in 2019. Its headquarters are in Muncie, Indiana, with a staff in the early 2020s of nearly fifty artists and licensing administrators.

In 1994, the company purchased all rights to the comic strips from 1978–93 from United Feature Syndicate, who owned the original black and white daily strips and original colour Sunday strips and retained their copyright. The full-colour daily strips and recoloured Sunday strips are copyrighted to Paws, Inc. as they are considered a different product. The strip is currently distributed by Universal Press Syndicate, while rights for the strip remain with Paws, Inc.

On 6 August 2019, it was announced that Nickelodeon and Paws, Inc. had come to a deal where Nickelodeon would buy the company and all of its productions, characters and trademarks. The deal did not include rights to the live action and direct-to-video Garfield movies, which are owned by Walt Disney Studios through its 20th Century Fox label after they acquired the rights in the 1990s before producing the two Garfield films in the 2000s. Of course, moving forward, Davis will continue to write and draw the comic strip with his production crew.

Paws, Inc. was founded by Davis as a creative house to support Garfield licensing. The company, located in rural Indiana, handles not only the creative angle, but also the business concerns of the corpulent kitty worldwide. Paws, Inc. is a privately held company and the sole owner of the copyrights and trademarks for Garfield and Garfield characters.

Davis guides the pencil that draws the comic strip, but he is also the guiding force at Paws, Inc. He is involved in the day-to-day running of the business and takes personal responsibility for shaping and growing Garfield, a character known and loved for more than forty years. Davis has a singular vision for Garfield and is always the last one to approve a design or comic strip. He has a big influence within the company, but a certain cat seems to hold more power.

'Take care of the cat and the cat will take care of you,' he has said on numerous occasions, and it seems that Garfield is the guiding light in the business. There are several overarching rules within Paws, Inc., and those include family coming first and having fun. At the heart of Paws, Inc., there seems to be a really affinity for what they have achieved with the character and a belief that being separated from corporate America in Muncie, Indiana, has really helped with their vision and their values as a company.

'We make every effort to provide the best service in the licensing industry,' says Davis. 'Having the creator and both the creative and business staff housed in one campus allows Paws to be flexible – there are no layers of management to cut through and no executive committees to slow things down.' Watching all they have accomplished, you can really appreciate that.

Chapter 9

The Commercialization of Garfield

Garfield is not just a comic strip, nor is it even merely a brand – it is a commercial empire, constructed by Davis and built under the name of Paws, Inc. The company's artists, administrators and managers are all in direct contact with the management of the orange cat. The company manages more than 400 licenses for its products, with interests in over 100 companies. Paws, Inc. is one of the most extensive businesses based in eastern Indiana.

Instead of licensing out his creation to other companies, Davis – with his strong background in marketing – decided to create Paws, Inc. to support the Garfield series, and has never looked back. Davis studied art and business at Bell State University in Indiana, and it seems that from the very beginning, he was just as committed to the entrepreneurial side as he was to the creative side.

According to Davis, one of the most iconic pieces of Garfield merchandise happened by accident:

'I designed the first "Stuck on You" doll with Velcro on the paws, thinking that people would stick it on curtains. It came back as a mistake with suction cups. They did not understand the directions. So I stuck it on a window and said, "If it's still there in two days, we'll approve this." Well, they were good suction cups and we released it like that. It never occurred to me that people would put them on cars.'

It's just the sort of happenstance that occurs a lot within the Garfield empire.

According to a 2004 article in the online magazine *Slate*, Garfield merchandise brought in between $750 million and $1 billion annually. Davis' creation has been adapted and licensed more times than anyone could probably count, but of all the products, there's one that Davis isn't overly enamoured with, as he explained during an interview:

'A few years ago there was a Zombie Garfield. It was *really* gnarly and I thought, "Oh, this will be fun." So I did it and it sold okay. It was really interesting. But then I looked at it later and I go, "It did nothing for the character's advancement." I figured I just did it because it was cool and everybody was doing it at the time. I just didn't have a warm, fuzzy feeling after doing it.

'If we take care of the cat, the cat will take care of us. There's not a profit motive or anything, it's actually, if you do something do it right.'

Garfield has had every single conceivable piece of merchandise, comic books, plush toys and cat food (obviously), but the strangest thing that Garfield ever licenced was … a musical. Yes, 'Garfield the Musical with Cattitude'. Davis was responsible for writing *Garfield Live*, while Michael Dansicker and Bill Meade handled the music and lyrics.

Davis has said of the plethora of Garfield merchandising:

'Doing plush [toys] allowed us to do them in 3D, so I got to turn them over and feel them and things like that. Doing the books was the perfect venue for continuing the comic strip behavior. Obviously the TV shows are great. The posters and cards, that's taking his attitude and doing really fun stuff with it. Doing office stuff just drives his personality further. He has the courage to say things people wish they could so they want stuff with him saying it so they don't have to. That kind of stuff helps drive the personality of the character.'

Garfield is still going strong, with a new racing game coming out and a constant stream of new merchandising. The amount of Garfield-related merchandise can certainly feel overwhelming, but Davis and Paws, Inc. paved the way for many independent companies to look at how to licence and market their property.

A Medium.com article claimed of Davis and the Garfield, 'Because success was the intended goal, the comic strip was simply the byproduct.'

While Davis never denies such claims or discussions, there is more to it than that when it comes to Garfield. Indeed, Paws, Inc. has held back merchandise at times due to concerns of oversaturation in the marketplace. Davis has further commented on the commercialization of Garfield:

'If I were to just rely on the comic strip and just do that, oh I'd probably be retired by now. I'd be a poor-handicapped golfer by now, but wouldn't have had nearly as much fun getting to this place. So, honestly, it wasn't so much the money as it was the challenge, the opportunity to do things. Just that part of me saying, "Hey if you wanna do it, you have to do it right."'

In many ways, Garfield represents the antithesis of Calvin and Hobbes. Arguably, Calvin and Hobbes was about exploration, about purpose and creativity, whereas Garfield never set out to do any of those things. Davis set out to do his own thing with Garfield, never intending to be profound, political or life-changing. The comic strip, character and story are designed to give you a laugh, to be a constant. The struggle with Garfield is that for something so long running, it's easier to make people laugh than give out daily pathos.

Garfield, Odie and Nermal all frequently appear at Silverwood Theme Park in northern Idaho. In the city of Athol, spread across 413 acres, is Silverwood Theme Park, home of Garfield's Summer Camp. It's the largest theme and water park in the American Northwest, with over seventy rides, several of them with a Garfield theme. It's not the only theme park with a Garfield slant: in 2019, China opened a Garfield theme park to allow visitors to experience the world of Garfield and his friends, with themed rides, attractions and live shows featuring the characters. The park is called Six Flags Zhejiang. Since being founded in 1974, Six Flags – an amusement park equally as popular as Disneyland and Universal Studios – now has twenty parks across the United States, Mexico and Canada.

This shows that the popularity of Garfield isn't restricted to the West; it extends worldwide. Perhaps the orange feline is even more beloved in China, as the whole theme park is dedicated to him. 'Garfield is already a beloved character in China and we look forward to bringing him to life inside Six Flags Zhejiang,' said Li Che, the chairman of the Riverside

Tourism Investment Group who organized the theme park deal with Paws, Inc.

Art Book

In 2016, Hermes Press signed an agreement with Paws, Inc. to publish a book on the art of author Jim Davis, titled *The Art of Jim Davis' Garfield*. The book includes an essay by author R.C. Harvey and other original material, and was released in July 2016 for the popular San Diego Comic-Con.

Restaurant

In 2018, a ghost restaurant themed after the franchise known as GarfieldEATS was opened in Dubai. The restaurant has been described by its founder and 'Chief Entergage Officer' (!) Nathen Mazri as a 'quick mobile restaurant', which is basically an app-based delivery service. Mazri claims that the restaurant is 'entergaging', a portmanteau of words presumably meaning 'entertaining' and 'engaging', which sounds interesting for a restaurant. Customers order food through the official mobile app, which also contains games and allows users to purchase episodes of *Garfield and Friends*. The restaurant serves lasagne (of course), Garfield-shaped pizza, 'Garfuccinos' and Garfield-shaped dark chocolate bars. A second location opened in Toronto in 2019. In an interview with FoodandWine.com, Mazri explained that it took seven months for a deal to be made, because 'it was a new concept and Jim Davis wanted to know more ... He said in 40 years, "Nobody has ever come to me with such a crazy idea."' And we don't doubt that at all.

Macy's Thanksgiving Day Parade

For those unaware, the Macy's Thanksgiving Day Parade is an annual tradition in New York City, presented by the department store Macy's. Macy's has been a staple in New York since 1858, a large department store in the heart of Manhattan. The parade usually marks the start of the run-in to Christmas, with the over-sized balloons in the parade often reflective of the trends in children's toys and popular culture. The parade features many helium air balloons, floats, live music and street performers. It has been an American institution since 1924 and has been televised on NBC since 1952, with an average of 44 million people in the US watching it each year. Garfield first appeared in the Macy's Thanksgiving Day Parade in 1983 as a costumed character on the America's Comic Stars float, along with several other iconic American comic characters, but it wasn't until a year later that he would get his own balloon. Along with a balloon resembling Raggedy Ann, the Garfield balloon was the first to be created by Raven Industries. The Garfield balloon was 60ft long, 35ft-wide, weighed 398lb and needed 18,907 cubic feet of helium to be fully inflated. The balloon featured Garfield sitting on all fours, resembling his older self, but with the big eyes people recognize.

The balloon of the lasagne-loving cat became a staple of the Macy's Thanksgiving Day Parade, appearing in six parades straight until 1989, even leading the parade in 1986 and 1988. He enjoyed a brief retirement between 1990 and 1991, then made his comeback in 1992 to celebrate his 15th birthday, and in 1993 once again led the parade. The balloon, which was always sponsored by Paws, Inc., made six further appearances until it was finally retired after the 1999 parade due to wear and tear. Garfield was often near the front of the balloon line-up, normally as the second balloon, highlighting the character's popularity. There has been speculation that the balloon still survives at the parade studio, but these are only rumours.

Davis has claimed that the Garfield balloon was one of the largest ever made:

'In the Macy's Thanksgiving Day Parade, they had published that their biggest balloon ever, by volume of gas, was Shamu the Whale with over 18,000 cubic feet. The fact is that the Garfield balloon was filled with 18,907 cubic feet of helium. So we just confirmed that the Garfield balloon, in fact, was the largest one by volume of gas.'

Whether this is true or not is unconfirmed.

In 2003, an all-new balloon of Garfield appeared as Macy's Holiday Ambassador to celebrate his 25th anniversary. This time he stood on two legs and carried his friend Pooky. Said to be the size of '37,000 pans of lasagna', this new balloon required 14,000 cubic feet of helium to fill it. Unlike the original balloon, this version appeared towards the end of the balloon line-up, as the last (2003 and 2006) or third-to-last (2004–05). The new balloon was retired after the 2006 parade, after making four appearances, giving Garfield a total of eighteen appearances in the Thanksgiving parade or a separate Christmas parade. Since then, a new Garfield balloon has yet to be introduced, though there is always time.

Garfield around the world

'When we were setting off we got so much interest in Britain, and I think that might be because I'm such a fan of British humour, that might have come through a bit. Benny Hill, Monty Python ... I love all that stuff. I mean, the Ministry of Silly Walks ... it doesn't get any funnier than that.'

Garfield's first foray into network television was with *The Fantastic Funnies*, a one-hour special on comic strips produced by Bill Meléndez and Lee Mendelson. It first aired on CBS on 15 May 1980.

The programme featured live-action segments, with Loni Anderson hosting and comic strip creators including Charles M. Schulz (Peanuts), Dik Browne (Hagar the Horrible), Hank Ketcham (Dennis the Menace) and Johnny Hart (B.C.) interviewed, but maybe the selling point was that it had animated sequences. *The Fantastic Funnies* showcased various comic strips, among them Peanuts, Hagar the Horrible, B.C., Broom-Hilda and Doonesbury. It was here that many comic strips came to life and gained new audiences. In the 1970s and 1980s, it was rare to get comic book characters across multi-media platforms like we see today, so *The Fantastic Funnies* was a unique way to see a character from a newspaper come to life in animation.

Host Loni Anderson introduced Garfield as a 'newcomer', being only two years old at the time. Most other strips featured on the show had many years behind them. The Garfield strip was represented with a brief animated scene. The segment includes adaptations of Garfield comic strips from (in order of appearance) 21 June 1978, 2 July 1979, 2 August 1978, 21 July 1978 and 12 May 1979. These featured Garfield failing to catch a mouse on Jon's orders; Garfield struggling to jump on the table;

Jon asking if Garfield has ever seen his feet; and Garfield getting an arm stuck in a jar trying to get the last olive. The strip is very basic, but it shows that there was something there to work with, and that even simply expanding the gags of the comic strip might actually work in a longer setting. But combining several strips into one animated short was only the beginning for Garfield the cat.

Chapter 10

Prime Time Specials

Here Comes Garfield

In 1982, Davis began production of the first television special, *Here Comes Garfield*, a thirty-minute show for CBS. It was at the time when *Garfield At Large* topped the *New York Times* bestseller list. It was directed by Phil Roman and featured Lorenzo Music as the voice of 'Garfield the house cat', as well as the voices of Sandy Kenyon, Henry Corden and Gregg Berger. *Here Comes Garfield* involved Garfield and Odie getting into mischief when they pester a neighbour's dog. The neighbour calls the animal control department from the City Pound, who arrive and capture Odie, who is too stupid to run away. Garfield runs off, but soon realizes that life without Odie is very boring, so decides to rescue him, but in doing so is captured himself. In the pound, he finds out from another dog that Odie is going to be euthanized. A girl then arrives, wanting to find a new pet, and she picks Garfield, but when the door opens all the animals run free and rescue Odie. They return to Jon's house, who thinks they were out having fun chasing cars while he was worrying about them. He gives Odie steak for breakfast and offers Garfield bacon and eggs, which he refuses, throwing them back in Jon's face.

The special was first broadcast on CBS on 25 October 1982. It was a ratings success, being watched by more than 50 million people, and was nominated for two Emmy Awards, including one for Outstanding Animated Program and one for director Phil Roman, who was nominated for the Outstanding Individual Achievement in Animated Programming. Ballantine Books also released a sixty-four-page adaptation of the special in September 1982.

It was in the making of this special that Garfield would change forever. The version of Garfield on all fours we had seen in the 1970s would dramatically transform into a more anthropomorphic version of the cat, who danced to the theme song in this special. In 1981, Davis had been working in a California studio on how to depict Garfield being able to dance, and it was proving a struggle. As in previous comics, the fictional cat always walked on all four feet. *Peanuts* creator Charles M. Schulz was in the same studio that day, and redrew Davis' work, advising him, 'The problem is, you've made Garfield's feet too small. Little tiny cat feet.' *Peanuts* TV special producers Bill Melendez and Lee Mendelson also produced *Here Comes Garfield*, a consequence of the two comic strips sharing the same syndicate, United Media.

One of the most popular American recording artists of the time, Lou Rawls, who had just completed a USO (United Service Organizations) tour at US Army bases, joined the project and released a soundtrack for it, recording the soundtrack in the summer of 1982. He explained, 'I figured if Bill Cosby could do *Fat Albert and the Cosby Kids* and live forever on the earnings, why can't I do *Garfield*?' The soundtrack was released by Epic Records the same year.

Davis wrote all the CBS Primetime specials and has fond memories of the old-school process of making them. Each one took about eight months to animate, done the old-fashioned way with hand-drawn animation. He recalled, 'They are just wonderful stories and I enjoy the memories of that time and the kind of faith that I think the network and producers and everyone had in our operation as far as being able to do the scripts and direct voice tracks and do the storyboards.'

Garfield on the Town

Garfield on the Town was the second Garfield special, and the first one to win a Primetime Emmy Award for Outstanding Animated Program. It was the last Garfield special that Roman directed before founding his own company, Film Roman,to produce the shows himself, starting with *Garfield in the Rough*, which was released in 1984.

The character of Jon Arbuckle was voiced by Sandy Kenyon in *Here Comes Garfield*, but was recast with Thom Huge for *Garfield on the Town*. Huge later voiced Jon in the remaining specials and much of the *Garfield and Friends* TV series.

The second special was originally aired on CBS on 28 October 1983 and was viewed by an estimated 40 million people. It has been rebroadcast in subsequent years. Ballantine Books again published a sixty-four-page illustrated adaptation the same year.

In *Garfield on the Town*, Jon suddenly becomes concerned about Garfield's behaviour after he and Odie mess up his house. While Jon tries to take him to the vet, Garfield accidentally falls out of Jon's car and later becomes lost downtown. After trying to find Jon, Garfield runs into a large gang of unfriendly alley cats known as the Claws. After antagonizing their leader, Garfield escapes into an abandoned Italian restaurant, where he is reunited with his long-lost mother, who tells him that the building was Garfield's birthplace and where he developed his love of lasagne. Meanwhile, Jon calls Garfield's vet, Dr Liz Wilson, to tell her about Garfield's disappearance, but Liz hangs up on him.

The next day, Garfield's mother takes him to see his extended family, including his tough maternal grandfather, his sickly half-brother Raoul and his cousin Sly, the latter of whom is the security guard on watch for the Claws gang. Garfield is appalled to learn that everyone in the family is a mouser. The Claws finally track Garfield down and surround the building, demanding that Garfield come out and face them. The family decides to fight the Claws instead of giving up Garfield to the gang. Garfield cowardly hides while his family fights and finally chase the gang away. Although Garfield is triumphant, his grandfather advises him to live with Jon instead as he is essentially useless with them. Reassured by his mother that they all envy his easy life at Jon's house, Garfield bids a sad farewell to his family and leaves.

Exhausted and hungry, Garfield walks alone in the street and it soon starts to rain. A car drives by and Garfield realizes it is being driven by Jon. Garfield chases after the car as fast as he can until he collapses onto the sidewalk and passes out. When Odie finally spots Garfield, unconscious, Jon pulls over to be reunited with him. Jon drives Garfield home and puts him into bed for the night. The next day, Garfield wakes up at Jon's house exhausted and ponders whether his entire experience was real or not. However, Garfield glimpses his mother looking at him through the window. She quickly disappears, while Garfield smiles and emotionally whispers, 'Thanks Mom, for everything.'

Featuring Garfield's mother made the special a poignant one. In the television specials, it seems that there was more room for experimentation and long-form storytelling for Garfield. They relied more on plot than cheap gags. A lot of the story revolves around Garfield being on his own, rather than using Odie or Jon to move the plot forward, and we learn something of Garfield's backstory.

Garfield in the Rough

The third special also won an Emmy in 1985, beating Snoopy's Getting Married, Charlie Brown and Donald Duck's 50th Birthday. It used plot devices such as Garfield talking to the audience that would become staples of Garfield for years to come For example, Garfield explains that the colour has gone out of his life and a subtitle comes up saying 'please do not adjust your television sets'.

The story begins with Jon agreeing with Garfield's prognosis that he's lost all the colour in his life and suggesting they take a vacation to help cure Garfield. With this revelation, the colour then suddenly comes back into Garfield's life and our screens. The big orange cat gets very excited that Jon wants to take him and Odie on vacation, starting to daydream about Acapulco in Mexico, Honolulu in Hawaii and Venice in Italy, which don't immediately seem like places Garfield would want to go, but then you realize the reason – the food! While each of the destinations has its negatives, mostly the effort Garfield needs to exert to get there, he seems happy enough to follow along. His excitement is quashed once Jon announces that they are going camping, with Jon forcing Garfield to go with him and Odie. Not quite Hawaii like Garfield had imagined!

This special marks another departure for Garfield, as he leaves the city, presumably for the first time. Almost immediately upon their arrival, a Park Ranger insults Garfield, thus putting him in a bad mood. Jon sets up his Super Delux tent and quickly falls foul to some pranks from Garfield, such as him mischievously putting a fish in the coffee pot. Unsurprisingly, our hero Garfield doesn't quite take to the outdoors like Jon and Odie, complaining that he would rather spend his time inside. When night falls, the three characters huddle in their cramped tent and listen to the radio, which is suddenly interrupted by a news report about a panther that has escaped from a local zoo that morning and has been reported to be in the Lake Woebegone area. After the news report, the announcer says, 'We now return to our regular broadcast of fun music.' The station then plays 'So Long Old Friend', a song from the first Garfield TV special – a nice touch. Upon hearing the news, a terrified Garfield wants to leave, but Jon assures him that Lake Woebegone (a possible reference to the fictional town of Lake Wobegon which was created by Garrison Keillor as a setting for his segment 'News from Lake Wobegon' which featured on the radio programme *A Prairie Home Companion*, broadcast from St Paul, Minnesota, from 1974 until 2016) is miles away from where they are and that they'll be fine. Following the announcement, Jon sings an old campfire song that his mother used to sing, 'Camping is my Life', to his two bemused pets, who wish to be anywhere else as Jon's singing is tantamount to torture. Just as the trio go into their tent to settle down and sleep for the night, on the hilltops behind them, the panther appears and growls as it eyes up the campsite.

The next day, Odie causes chaos by licking Jon's feet at dawn, which causes the tent to roll down the hillside into the lake. Odie runs away after Garfield tells him to go and eat something poisonous. Odie runs into the woods and we see a sign that tells us the lake they fell into is really Lake Woebegone and that Jon was trying to protect his pets by telling them not to worry. Garfield and Odie's relationship is always fractious, which is never clearer than when Odie is causing havoc for Garfield.

The forest rangers hunting for the panther find Jon's tent and go to warn him to evacuate the area, but finding no one there, they leave him a note and move on swiftly. However, a gust of wind subsequently tosses the message into the campfire, where it catches fire and disintegrates. Jon discovers that both Garfield and Odie have eaten their entire supply of food for the week and starts ranting at Garfield, blaming him. After this, Garfield heads through the woods to escape Jon's rants. While there, he starts to appreciate the great outdoors for a brief moment until he meets two forest animals, Dicky Beaver and Billy Bunny, who warn Garfield about the panther Garfield heard about on the radio. The two forest creatures claim that the panther has already attacked other animals. Odie emerges from the dense forest, after initially accidentally scaring Garfield away, and the pair eavesdrop on two rangers passing by with a large tranquilizer gun, attempting to shoot the panther. The rangers discuss their plan, with one slightly more worried than the other, thinking that a tranquilizer gun isn't enough to stop the wild beast. Garfield and Odie, brought closer together by their predicament, decide that they need to find Jon and leave before they are attacked – or worse – by the beast, and they run back to the campsite, realizing they won't get far without Jon, no matter how much Garfield hates him at times.

When they return, Garfield acts frantically, trying to warn Jon, but Jon obviously doesn't understand him: Garfield is no Lassie! Jon insists that they have some dried fruit and refuses to move from the campsite, determined to make the holiday a success in typical Jon fashion Garfield turns his attention to Odie and tries to get him into the car, warning him that they will end up dead if they don't leave right away. As the late afternoon gives way to evening, the full moon comes into view, like in an old Hammer Horror film, shining down on the camp and forest. We see that the panther has crept into the campsite and is approaching the trio, who can only look on in horror, frozen, not knowing what to do. Invoking some deep-down feline behaviour, Garfield escapes up a tree – which is very unlike him. Meanwhile, Jon and Odie hide in the tent, but quickly switch to Jon's car when the panther tears the tent apart with ease. The beast then smashes through the car window. Scared, but unable to just watch Jon and Odie in peril, Garfield leaps from the tree and bravely takes on the panther, clawing at its head and neck, only to be shaken off. Maybe Garfield does care after all. Jon and Odie then try to shield Garfield from the irate animal. In the nick of time, the park rangers enter the campsite and take down the panther by putting him to sleep with a tranquilizer dart. Jon congratulates Garfield for being a hero, in shock at the panther and at Garfield's heroics. The rangers tell Jon that they were heroes too for handling the panther and putting themselves in harm's way. If the rangers hadn't made it there on time, or if they had missed their shot at the panther, then Garfield, Jon and Odie would all have been done for.

Jon feels they have had enough adventure and recommends they break camp and return to the relatively safety and calmness of home, which is music to Odie and Garfield's ears. The rangers return the panther to the zoo under lock and key, while Garfield, Jon and Odie set off for home, with Garfield acting like an excited child, retelling the story of how he took on the panther, as well as struggling to get the phrase, 'When the going gets tough, the tough get going' right. Garfield finds himself as the unlikely hero in this adventure. This special shows that Garfield is actually equipped to help out and deal with danger. While he doesn't act with such motivation in his day-to-day life, it shows that there is more to

Garfield than meets the eye and that despite what he says, he does care for his friends.

Garfield's Halloween Adventure

Garfield's Halloween Adventure – which was originally going to be titled *Garfield in Disguise*, until it was decided that having Halloween in the title would be more exciting – first aired on CBS on 30 October 1985 to coincide with Halloween. Much like other Halloween cartoon staples such as *The Halloween Tree* and *It's The Great Pumpkin, Charlie Brown*, it has often beenrepeated around the same time each year. It won the Primetime Emmy Award for Outstanding Animated Program, defeating other illustrious competition… Garfield himself in *Garfield in Paradise*. It was also the subject of an illustrated children's book adaptation. The theme song for *Garfield's Halloween Adventure* is 'This Is The Night', about getting candy on Halloween night. 'This is the night I was created for', the song goes, which is perfect for Garfield, getting free candy for doing very little.

Garfield wakes early in the morning to the obnoxious *Binky the Clown Show* on TV, informing him that today is Halloween. Garfield, being a cat, idly lets the days pass him by without a care in the world, but this one is different. He becomes overexcited about trick-or-treating, losing himself in the moment, thinking about all the food. Eventually, Garfield manages to trick Odie into believing that dogs are required to trick-or-treat with cats and give them almost all of their candy, leaving very little for the dogs. Odie is tempted, even by the minimal reward – showing his stupidity – and the pair head for the attic to find costumes in one of Jon's old trunks. After considering several options, Garfield decides he and Odie will be pirates.

As they are about to head out, Jon gives them sacks and tells them to have a good time trick-or-treating and not be out too late, like they are his children. Garfield and Odie then head out, blending in amongst the children in their neighbourhood. Again, the place and time is never mentioned in Garfield, adding to the generational appeal of the cartoon, giving it a timeless quality. Odie quickly starts to show fear at all the spooky characters he is seeing, while Garfield reassures him that they are only children in costumes. To try to reassure his scared dog brother,

Garfield goes to lift some of the costumes, only to find there aren't children under some of them, but rather terrifying looking ghosts. Arriving at a dock, Garfield decides to cross the river on a rowboat to escape some of the scary looking people he sees and to visit more houses in the hope of getting extra candy for himself. When Garfield tells Odie to put out the oars, Odie doesn't understand the instruction and throws the oars overboard. This leaves a furious Garfield to stew as he can do nothing while the boat drifts down the river, further away from any candy.

After some time, the boat comes to a standstill near a creaky old dock connected to a dilapidated mansion. The scaredy-cat and dog think that the mansion is deserted and go inside, but are startled to find an old man rocking in a chair. As they get to know him, the old man tells them a story that exactly 100 years ago, pirates buried their treasure under the floor of the mansion and signed a blood oath to return for the treasure at midnight a century later, even though it meant that they would rise from their graves. He tells them was a 10-year-old cabin boy who worked for the pirates at the time. Concerned and utterly terrified, Garfield and Odie start to leave, backing away. Garfield asks the old man if he wants to come too, being kind, but he has disappeared, stealing their boat and leaving the pair behind in the abandoned mansion

When the old longcase clock in the house chimes midnight, Garfield and Odie watch as a ghostly ship appears through fog on the river, and pirate ghosts emerge from the water in front of them. Garfield and Odie retreat to an empty kitchen cupboard as the ghosts come to collect their buried treasure from the creaking floorboards of the house. However, when Odie sneezes thanks to layers of dust in the old mansion, it alerts the ghosts to their hiding place. Garfield and Odie jump into the river to escape, Odie rescuing Garfield as he cannot swim and dragging him to the safety of the riverbank. When they wash ashore, they find their boat with all their candy still inside and mysteriously untouched. They go home happy and Garfield repays Odie's rescue by reluctantly giving him his fair and rightful share of all their spoils from trick-or-treating. Afterwards, Garfield turns on the TV, only to see the old man wearing his pirate hat and hosting an all-night pirate movie marathon. Garfield turns off the TV and goes to bed.

This is another of Garfield's more outlandish stories that feature that element of 'did that really happen to Garfield or did he just imagine it in a crazy dream?'.

Davis has said that he intended the special to begin on a familiar tone, then 'go somewhere that would at least scare 4-year-olds'. That has always been the appeal of Garfield, something that doesn't push the boundaries too far, so that it doesn't lose its appeal and values for kids, while parents and other adults can still watch and appreciate it. There is a craftsmanship and beauty to the animation in *Garfield's Halloween Adventure*, which is a perfect example of the Garfield shows often being a pastiche on American culture. Davis also said of the setting, 'The only way I could do that was to get [Garfield and Odie] away from the house and the neighborhood – so that's what the boat represented: if they lost control and then the boat took them somewhere else.' He felt that the only way he could create some horror and dread was to remove Garfield and Odie from the relative safety of their home neighbourhood. It is a familiar feeling for any child who has been lost.

C. Lindsay Workman was cast as the voice of the old man in the spooky house, having previously voiced Garfield's grandfather in *Garfield on the Town*. Producer Lee Mendelson chose Workman, wanting someone with a deep, booming voice and gravitas. Most of the Garfield actors would get regular work on the show, and it seems the producers were very loyal to guest actors, often giving them new roles in different specials through the years.

Davis recalled of the making of the Halloween special:

'It was such a challenge to try to think of something that could be scary, but fortunately we got to work with animation. We could marry scary sounds with scary music and scary images, and set the stage for a scary experience. C. Lindsay Workman was just a great character actor. I think we took our time to build to a scary scene where the ghost pirates invaded the house to look for the buried treasure. We tried to throw as many elements together as possible to create a situation where, at least for a few minutes, it could create a scary situation for the young viewers.'

Under the original title *Garfield in Disguise*, the show was premiered on CBS in 1985 along with the 1966 Peanuts special *It's the Great Pumpkin,*

Charlie Brown. In later years, it was often aired in the Halloween season with *It's the Great Pumpkin, Charlie Brown*. By 2015, *Garfield's Halloween Adventure* was no longer broadcast as frequently on American network television.

A sixty-four-page illustrated book adaptation was published in 1985 by Random House Publishing Group, originally under the title *Garfield in Disguise* but later retitled *Garfield's Halloween Adventure*. The book adaptation deviates in only a few ways from the TV show. First, it adds a scene with Garfield telling Odie a little about the history of Halloween, with its origins as a seventh-century Druid festival celebrating the day of Samhain, Lord of Death. The book also implies that the old man himself is a ghost, and their boat is merely pulled away by the current instead of being stolen by him. Finally, an extra sequence is included in which Garfield takes a ring from the treasure and is followed home by the pirate ghosts until he returns the stolen item.

The special was included on the DVD *The Garfield Holiday Collection* on 4 November 2014, sold exclusively by Walmart, and was also made available for digital download on 11 November that year.

Garfield in Paradise

Garfield in Paradise is an animated television special directed by Phil Roman. This, the fifth Garfield animated special, originally aired on CBS on 27 May 1986, with special guest star Wolfman Jack playing the tribal chief. Jack was one of America's most popular DJs, known for his gravelly voice and unique energy. Jack featured in numerous films and television shows down the years, perhaps most notably as himself in the George Lucas movie *American Grafitti*. Davis was excited to work with Jack on the special, explaining, 'It was just way fun. We did it for silliness.' This show was the final credit on Garfield for Frank Nelson, who once again portrayed a variation on his recurring character from *The Jack Benny Program*. He would die in September of the same year as *Garfield in Paradise* was first aired.

In this special, the story follows Jon and Garfield taking a third-class airline trip to Paradise World, a cheapskate version of Hawaii, really giving you a sense of Jon's character, skimping on everything. When they arrive on the island, Jon and Garfield check in at a near abandoned moltel and soon discover that there is no beach anywhere near, and only an empty swimming pool, leading to a crushing sense of disappointment for both Jon and Garfield. When they enter their room, Jon opens his suitcase to find Odie hiding there. Garfield, Jon and Odie are bored in their room and around the pool, until Jon formulates a plan. Renting a car, the three drive off in search of a beach. They hire a classic Chevrolet Bel Air and begin to cruise around the island, finally feeling like they are on holiday, but the car then mysteriously speeds into the jungle on its own volition, stopping at a native village. Jon, Garfield and Odie fear they are in danger until the natives begin kowtowing to the car. They meet the tribal chief (The High Ramma-Lamma), who explains that the villagers (The Ding-Dongs) learned English from watching lots of 1950s beach movies. The chief and his villagers are named after the 1957 hit song 'Rama Lama Ding Dong' by doo-wop group The Edsels. In 1957 (the same year as the song) a man known as the Cruiser – who bears a striking resemblance to movie star James Dean or Fonz from *Happy Days* – drove his car into the village and introduced the people to 1950s pop culture. When a nearby volcano began to erupt, threatening the village, the Cruiser saved their homes by driving his car into the volcano, preventing it from erupting and destroying the whole area. The village and its inhabitants are now devoted to the 1950s teenage lifestyle, as seen in movies like *American Graffitti* and *Grease*. The tribal chief believes that Jon's rental car is the same one that the Cruiser owned.

Jon starts a romance with tribal princess Owooda, and Garfield finds friendship with her cat, Mai-Tai. Meanwhile, the chief demands Monkey, who is seen as the village idiot, to fix the car for Jon, with the help (or hinderance) of Odie. However, the volcano begins to erupt and Owooda tells Jon that she and Mai-Tai must sacrifice themselves to save the village from disaster. The volcano rejects Owooda and Mai-Tai, the village Shaman, Pigeon, seeing this as a sign that it wants the car instead; if the volcano does not have the car immediately, it will destroy the island. Monkey and Odie make a final attempt to fix the car, which still does not work until Odie gives distributor cap a hit with a hammer. The car then finally starts, speeding through the village. It takes off and up the side of the volcano, with Monkey at the wheel but not really driving and Odie hanging onto the car's bonnet. Plummeting into the volcano, the car disappears and the volcano finally erupts. The spirit of the Cruiser himself and his car drift into the night sky. Pigeon claims that the volcano has finally been appeased. Worried for Monkey and Odie, the villagers fear the worst until Garfield sees them climb out of the crater with barely a scratch. Jon and Garfield carry Odie and Monkey down the mountain and back to the village, where they are given a hero's welcome.

Davis identified *Garfield in Paradise* as 'absolutely one of my favorites. It's bright, funny, [there's] rock 'n' roll in it.' That certainly comes across for viewers, as Davis and the animators again take Garfield out of his comfort zone, playing with bright colour schemes, new themes and a lot of music. *Garfield in Paradise* plays on the 1950s psyche, with lots of details and nods to the music of the decade, an idyllic time that features heavily in American culture. *Garfield in Paradise* is thus one of the most notable specials, with its memorable side characters, unique setting and story, as well as some of the most endearing music from any special. Those songs included the popular 'Hello, Hawaii (Can I Come Over)' performed by Lou Rawls and Desiree Goyette, 'Beauty and the Beach' by Rawls, Thom Huge and Lorenzo Music, and 'When I Saw You' by Huge and Desiree Goyette. It should also be noted that Jon actually falls in love and, for once, his advances are not rejected. Ballantine Books released a children's book which covered most of the same story as this special in the same year.

Garfield Goes Hollywood

This special was first broadcast on CBS on 8 May 1987, and was nominated for Outstanding Animated Program at the 39th Primetime Emmy Awards.

Garfield and Odie believe their dance routines, performed on top of the neighbourhood fences, cannot be beaten, and Jon thinks the same. They happen to be watching *Pet Search* (a pets' version of the talent show *Star Search*) when they come up with an idea of entering the show. Jon is hoping to win the $1,000 prize, which Garfield is unimpressed with. They perform as an Elvis-style trio called 'Johnny Bop and the Two-Steps'. Neither Odie nor Garfield want Jon involved in their act, thinking he's awful at singing, performing and everything else! Garfield is also embarrassed because they have to wear kitsch 1950s-era costumes and sing like Elvis.

Despite their awful act, they win the regional competition (a dog that plays five instruments simultaneously is disqualified when Odie exposes him as a man in a canine costume) and are able to compete at the national finals in Hollywood, staying at a swanky Beverly Hills hotel. Garfield and Odie, fearing their act is too mediocre to win, destroy Jon's guitar. Jon, seeing his wrecked instrument, is heartbroken. However, it allows Garfield and Odie to come up with a better act for the show.

The *Pet Search* finals have a host named Burt and an announcer named Bob. Bob tells Burt the winner will receive $1 million, with the runner-up winning a boat. While Jon, Garfield and Odie watch the other competitors, Jon tells them that even though they were happy they won the local *Pet Search* contest and $1,000, made it to Hollywood and now wanted to take the massive cash prize, he thinks that Garfield and Odie should lose the final on purpose and return to their old lives as a prize of their own. Garfield disagrees, and he and Odie compete as a tango-dancing duo called 'The Dancing Armandos', winning the boat for second place and only losing out on the top prize to an opera-singing cat. Angry over losing, Garfield destroys the set, but Jon reassures him that they still won the boat. The special ends back home, where Garfield finally admits to Jon that it was all for the best that they are home again: they are on their boat fantasizing about sailing to exotic locations, despite living in a landlocked town and having to settle for sitting on it in their backyard.

A Garfield Christmas

In this 1987 festive special, Garfield dreams that he is woken by Jon dressed as an elf, who feeds him a large dish of lasagna before giving him his gift, a robotic Santa Claus which reads minds and produces whatever the user wants. When Jon actually wakes up Garfield, he tells him that it is Christmas Eve morning, and they and Odie are going to the countryside to celebrate Christmas with Jon's family on their farm. Garfield is annoyed that they always go to the farm and the family never come to Jon's house. During his drive to the farm, Jon talks about Christmases from his youth, with his parents, brother Doc Boy and Grandma, while Garfield listens with great cynicism.

Upon arrival, Jon's Grandma and Garfield quickly form a close bond. While Jon, Garfield and Odie take a walk, Grandma spikes Mom's sausage gravy with chilli powder, bragging that her gravy just won the Greene County Fair. Jon and Garfield return for dinner, while Odie works on something secretive and then sneaks back into the house. After dinner, they decorate the Christmas tree. Jon asks Garfield to put the star on, as no one else can reach the top of the tree. As the family sings festive songs, Grandma tells Garfield about her beloved deceased husband, whom she especially misses at Christmas because of his unspoken, but obvious, love for the holiday. Mom later asks Dad to read a book called *Binky: The Clown Who Saved Christmas*. Dad is reluctant, tired of reading it every year, but he gives in. That night, Garfield notices Odie acting suspiciously and follows him to the barn, seeing Odie making something out of wood, wire, a plunger handle and a hand rake. Garfield stumbles upon some old letters, realizing they must be over fifty years old.

On Christmas morning, when it seems like all the presents have been opened, Garfield gives Grandma the letters he found in the barn. These were love notes written to Grandma by her husband when they first met. Garfield finds out that Odie has been busy making his ultimate Christmas gift: a homemade back scratcher for his feline brother. Garfield thanks and embraces Odie for the gift. This is a rare glimpse at Garfield's other side, as he learns the true meaning of Christmas: 'It's not the giving, it's not the getting, it's the loving!'

Davis based the story on experiences he had celebrating Christmas with his family on their farm in Indiana, with many of the Arbuckles modelled on the Davis family. Davis' real-life brother was known as Doc Boy. Davis referred to the story as 'very autobiographical', adding, 'That was *my* Christmas on the farm.' However, he said that Grandma was an entirely fictional character, added for the emotional subplot of having time with loved ones at Christmas.

The episode first aired on 21 December 1987. According to online magazine *Bustle*, the Garfield festive special was rebroadcast every year until 2000, an impressive feat for an animated special, revealing just how big Garfield's reach in animation was. The programme was often shown alongside the 1965 Peanuts special *A Charlie Brown Christmas*.

Happy Birthday, Garfield

Happy Birthday, Garfield is an hour-long television special dedicated to the tenth anniversary of the Garfield comic strip, hosted by Jim Davis. The special was first broadcast on 17 May 1988 on CBS. It featured a very brief 1980 animated short from *The Fantastic Funnies* (two years before *Here Comes Garfield*) by Bill Melendez and Lee Mendelson, featuring jokes from the comic strips of 21 June and 2 August 1978 and 7 July 1979, as well as behind-the-scenes footage and anecdotes from Davis to celebrate Garfield's birthday.

The special featured a rare glimpse of a recording session for the upcoming *Garfield and Friends* series (with Lorenzo Music, Gregg Berger and Thom Huge), along with some 'sneak peak' footage from it and *Garfield: His 9 Lives*.

Other highlights included Spanish and German-dubbed clips of *Here Comes Garfield* and *Garfield Goes Hollywood*, showing that Garfield's reach was already pretty much worldwide. It was also notable for a 'sneak peek' at the unproduced feature film *Garfield's Judgement Day* and a rehearsal for the theme song of upcoming special *Garfield's Babes and Bullets*.

Towards the end of the special, Davis talks with fellow comic creators including Dik Browne (Hägar the Horrible, Hi and Lois), Mike Peters (Mother Goose and Grimm) and Lynn Johnston (For Better or For Worse). The final part of the programme features the celebrations held for the comic strip's anniversary, notably where fellow cartoonists draw their characters as 'presents', followed by interviews about Garfield from people in the street, before we are shown Garfield and Odie (played, strangely, by humans) living the high life in Hollywood. Finally, Davis acknowledges the audience before setting off on a Garfield-shaped hot air balloon. It's a very surreal ending to the show, which stands out in the series of specials for being a one-off, where we see Davis and other creators talk about the importance of Garfield.

Garfield: His 9 Lives

This hour-long television special was partly an adaptation of a book, and partly new segments created entirely for the series. It was produced in 1988 and featured ten separate segments, just like the book of the same name, which was released in 1984. Six of these segments were adapted from the book, with the other four newly written for the show by Davis himself. 'Babes and Bullets' was adapted into a television special of its own, *Garfield's Babes and Bullets*, the following year, and won an Emmy Award for Outstanding Animated Program of 1989. 'The Vikings', 'The Exterminators' and 'Primal Self' were stories from the original His 9 Lives book that have never been adapted for television. The special is included on the DVD *Garfield's Fantasies*, and was the eighth of twelve Garfield television specials made between 1982 and 1991. The segments were as follows:

'In the Beginning' (directed by Phil Roman): God orders that the cat be created according to his specifications. Unlike the rest of the special, this prologue sequence is shot in live-action. The scene where the angels question why God gives cats nine lives varies slightly from the storybook version. God's feline features are not seen – yet; he simply states that it might make a 'great plot for a story'.

'Cave Cat' (directed by Phil Roman and George Singer): Garfield says, 'In my first life, I formulated many of my likes and dislikes. I disliked my rock bed. On the other hand, you wouldn't believe the size of the Pteradon drumsticks.' Evolution takes place as, 10 million years ago, a cat first swims out of the sea into its Neanderthal-like state. The segment is full of comedic sketches depicting primitive life characteristics, including a hunting routine and the first steps in learning how to talk.

'King Cat' (directed by Phil Roman and John Sparey): '2000 BC was a good year to be a cat in Egypt,' says Garfield. 'We were revered, even worshipped. Ah, for the good old days.' In Ancient Egypt, the Pharaoh's sacred cat discovers what happens to him if the Pharaoh dies. King Cat must try to defend the king from his evil brother to prevent this fate. This was the first of the new segments introduced in the special. Since cats were worshipped in Ancient Egypt, it was in this life where Garfield developed his love for being pampered.

'In the Garden' (directed by Phil Roman and Ruth Kissane): 'My third life was my favourite,' Garfield tells us. 'My body grew old, but I never, never, never grew up.' A young kitten who looks like a stripe-less Garfield and its human companion have a happy life dancing in a dream-like garden, but are tempted by a mysterious box that can never be opened. Filled with surreal elements, the segment ends exploring the idea of curiosity and how it may lead to an unknown (and maybe inconvenient) path.

'Court Musician' (directed by Bob Scott): Garfield says, 'I learned to think on my feet in my fourth life. Thinking was okay, I guess, but now I avoid it whenever possible.' In 1720, the king demands a concerto from 'Freddie' Handel, and it better be a good one. Under the pressure of a deadline and a jester who wants him to fail, 'Freddie' delegates the concerto's finale to his pet, one of Garfield's incarnations, a blue cat. Like 'King Cat', this segment and the following two were created specifically for television.

'Stunt Cat' (directed by Phil Roman, Bill Littlejohn and Bob Nesler): 'Life No. 5 was short ...' we are told. Garfield is (briefly) a stunt double for Krazy Kat. According to Garfield, his life as a stunt double was his shortest.

'Diana's Piano' (directed by Doug Frankel): 'Six must be my lucky number, because that's the life I fell in love with music,' Garfield says. 'I also fell in love with a girl who played the piano just for me.' A young girl, Sara, receives a cat, Diana, who goes with her everywhere, especially to piano lessons. This is the only one of Garfield's lives, in either the book or special, where the cat is explicitly identified as female. The story is told in flashback, with the animation reminiscent of watercolour paintings. It is closer than any of the others to reality; the cat, Diana, is just a normal cat.

'Lab Animal' (directed by Phil Roman and Doug Frankel): 'In my seventh life, I was a laboratory animal,' says Garfield. 'To this day, every time I see a test tube, I throw up.' Test animal 19-GB makes a daring escape to avoid dissection. His appearance was similar to that of Oliver from *Oliver & Company*, and the story and animation were similar to *The Plague Dogs* (adapted from the story by *Watership Down* author Richard Adams) and German adult animated mystery *Felidae*. Garfield's commentary varies slightly from the book, saying that he becomes nauseous at the sight of scientific equipment rather than medical equipment.

'Garfield' (directed by Phil Roman, John Sparey and Bob Nesler): Garfield says, 'All that I ever was made me what I am in my eighth life. Somehow it's falling short of my expectations.' This segment is a prequel to *Garfield on the Town*. Dating back to 1978, Garfield is born and taken in by Jon, who then buys Odie.

'Space Cat' (directed by Phil Roman, John Sparey and Bob Nesler): 'I'd like to think I'll live forever, but hey, I'm only human,' says Garfield. 'Here's a sneak preview of my ninth life.' Garfield and Odie try to retaliate when the IHGWF (Incredibly Huge Galactic War Fleet, led by 'Commander Mendelson', named after producer Lee Mendelson) threatens to destroy them. Garfield and Odie are killed at the end of this life, and meet God in the afterlife. Because the odds were so unfairly stacked against Garfield and Odie (and because God hadn't been able to keep track of the lives Garfield had lived through due to heaven's computers being down at the time), the pair are given all nine lives back. After they vanish, the special concludes when God, with his cat-like eyes now visible, says, 'We have to stick together, you know.'

From 2014–15, BOOM Studios adapted *His 9 Lives* across four comics, with each story drawn by a different artist. It can be seen as a hybrid of the book and the special as, like the special, it features several lives created exclusively for it, and remains a favourite amongst fans. Garfield's eighth life, the current one, is also left out altogether, with each life's prologue instead being set during the eighth life.

Garfield's Babes & Bullets

Garfield's Babes and Bullets aired on 23 May 1989 on CBS. The special won that year's Primetime Emmy Award for Outstanding Animated Program (One Hour or Less). The animated version of *Garfield: His 9 Lives* was also nominated. It features Lorenzo Music as the voice of Garfield, reimagined as private detective Sam Spayed (a spoof of Humphrey Bogart's Sam Spade from *The Maltese Falcon*) attempting to solve a murder mystery. Music's drab voice perfectly fits the noir private detective character.

The story begins with a bored Garfield investigating a closet, finding a trench coat and fedora hat. Trying on both, he fantasizes that he is Sam Spayed, a second-rate private investigator in a 1940s film noir. Sam receives a visit from the beautiful Tanya O'Tabby, who hires him to investigate the death of her husband, Professor O'Tabby, who apparently drove off a clifftop. Tanya believes it was murder, as her husband was an excellent driver, but the death was ruled an accident. Despite initially suspecting foul play (that Tanya killed her husband for his money or because he was unfaithful), Sam takes on the case.

No solid proof of murder comes to light when Sam visits the morgue, although he notes that the professor's shirt, chest and stomach hairs have yellowish-brown stains on them, and secretly takes a mysterious painted stone that the coroner overlooked. Sam then visits the university where O'Tabby worked and meets his colleague and former advisor Professor O'Felix. He tells Sam that O'Tabby was on his way to visit an elderly benefactress the night he died, but dismisses Sam's idea that the professor was having an affair, saying his one weakness was a coffee addiction.

Sam phones Tanya to tell her what he has discovered, only for his newly hired secretary Kitty to spill coffee on him when he mentions talking to O'Felix about O'Tabby's 'woman trouble'. While cleaning himself up, Sam realizes that the 'stone' is actually a ceramic fragment from a broken coffee mug and the stains on the late professor's clothing and body must have been coffee. He deduces that Kitty previously worked for O'Tabby, and accuses her of his murder, her motive being that her love for the professor was not reciprocated. Kitty breaks down in tears, insisting that she did not kill the professor and left the university because she was unable to bear not having him. She explains that she did more than make coffee for O'Tabby, also filling in his prescriptions for potent sleeping pills to counter his coffee-induced insomnia.

Deducing O'Felix is the murderer, Sam brings him to court. O'Felix was jealous of his former student's success and murdered him by spiking his coffee with sleeping pills, causing him to fall asleep at the wheel and drive off the cliff. Tanya visits Sam one last time, making it clear that the romance he had hoped to have with her will never happen. Kitty starts to seduce Sam, only for reality to intrude as Jon Arbuckle asks Garfield what he's up to in the closet.

Garfield's Babes and Bullets is perhaps one of the strangest homages to Dashiell Hammett's creation Sam Spade, but is nevertheless very entertaining, maybe one of Garfield's finest appearances. It proved enormously popular and remains a fans' favourite.

Garfield's Thanksgiving

This special was first broadcast on CBS on 22 November 1989 and was nominated for Outstanding Animated Program at the 42nd Primetime Emmy Awards. The songs featured in *Garfield's Thanksgiving* include 'Make Thanksgiving One Whole Meal' by Lou Rawls and 'It's a Quiet Celebration' by Desirée Goyette.

Garfield and Odie scare Jon out of bed with military music, pretending to be drill sergeants, demanding pancakes 'the size of Australia' and plenty of coffee for breakfast. Garfield then decides to take a nap but changes his mind to kick Odie off the table. Along the way, Garfield checks the calendar and discovers to his horror that he has an appointment with the vet. He removes the date, hoping to make Jon forget, but notices that tomorrow is Thanksgiving so demands Jon buy the holiday food. On the way home from the supermarket, Jon remembers the vet appointment; Garfield screams all the way there.

While at the vets, Dr Liz Wilson examines Garfield as Jon tries to talk her into going on a date with him. Liz tells Garfield he is too fat and must be put on a diet, but is otherwise healthy. She tells Jon what the diet is composed of, causing Garfield to panic. Liz reluctantly agrees to the date with Jon, who invites her to his house for Thanksgiving dinner.

Back home, Jon is excited that Liz is coming for Thanksgiving, but Garfield is miserable at being on a diet. After eating half a leaf of lettuce for lunch, Garfield tries to raid the fridge, but is stopped by Odie, whom Jon has assigned to ensure Garfield doesn't cheat on his diet. Garfield weighs himself on his talking scales, but destroys them for comparing him to Orson Welles. He is repeatedly foiled by Odie when he tries to steal cookies, flour, salt and sugar. Garfield wonders if the lack of food is making him hallucinate.

On Thanksgiving morning, Garfield is even grumpier than usual as Jon prepares the special meal. Jon has no idea how to prepare the dinner: he didn't thaw the turkey overnight, doesn't bother to make stuffing, rubs butter on his skin instead of the turkey's, and roasts it at 500 degrees Fahrenheit instead of 325. Garfield helps ruin the meal further by putting garlic powder in the vegetables. Jon shaves and picks a suit, but when Liz arrives she notices he forgot to put on any trousers. As Jon goes to check on the meal, Liz inspects Garfield and wonders if she was a too harsh on him with the diet. Garfield pretends to be suffering from every single withdrawal symptom Liz mentions, so she lets him off the diet, instantly cheering him up until he realizes he'll have to eat Jon's food.

In the kitchen, Jon is faced with a still frozen turkey and the realization that he hasn't a clue how to prepare a Thanksgiving lunch. Garfield convinces Jon to call Grandma, who arrives seconds later and gets Jon out of the kitchen. As Jon distracts Liz by giving her a history lesson about Thanksgiving, Grandma cooks the meal: she slices the turkey with a chainsaw, adds white sauce, then batters and deep fries the slices into her famous turkey croquettes, prepares sweet potatoes by covering them with butter, brown sugar and marshmallows, and finishes with 'split-second cranberry sauce' and pumpkin pie. Once everything is ready, Grandma tells Garfield that Liz could not have found a better man than Jon, then asks Garfield to eat a piece of pie for her as she leaves.

Garfield tells Jon, who has bored Liz to sleep with his stories, that everything is ready. After the meal, Liz declares that the food was wonderful and agrees to come back next year, then thanks Jon for inviting her with a kiss on the cheek before leaving. Jon, Garfield and Odie declare it was a great day and are thankful for Grandma. They decide to go for a walk to work off the meal, but Odie is too bloated from overeating to get off the couch. Jon puts Odie on a diet, and Garfield gleefully torments Odie into doing push-ups as payback for his earlier brutality.

Garfield's Feline Fantasies

The special was first broadcast on 18 May 1990 on CBS and was nominated for Outstanding Animated Program at the 42nd Primetime Emmy Awards. The eleventh of twelve Garfield specials made between 1982 and 1991, it is the only one not to feature Lou Rawls.

Garfield's fantasy life is beginning to take over his real life, a la Walter Mitty. He keeps slipping into a fantasy world, sometimes without warning. In these fantasies, which compose the bulk of the special, he becomes Lance Sterling, an amalgamation of James Bond and Indiana Jones. With his associate Slobberjob (Odie, inspired by Bond villain Oddjob), he travels to exotic locations such as Istanbul, Paris, and the Amazon rainforest to find the Banana of Bombay and lay claim to it before his enemy Fat Guy gets to it. On the way they meet a mysterious Moldavian lady named Nadia, who has an agenda of her own.

Garfield is dreaming about being a submarine captain, with Pooky as his commanding officer. When Garfield's alarm clock wakes him up, Garfield continues the dream's storyline and fires a torpedo, smashing the clock. Garfield enters a cowboy fantasy when greeting Odie and a magician fantasy when waking up Jon to make them breakfast. Odie joins him in the latter fantasy.

Garfield tells Odie their fantasies are not dangerous as Jon is always there to bail them out. They test this theory by entering a fantasy where they are pilots of a jet plane with faulty engines. When Jon saves them from falling, they decide the theory is correct and climb into the fridge, entering another fantasy.

Garfield becomes Lance Sterling, with Odie as bodyguard Slobberjob. The two travel to an Asian city and meet villain Fat Guy and his bodyguard Rameet. It is revealed Lance and Slobberjob have been sent to find the Banana of Bombay, the first banana used in the banana-peel gag. However, it disappeared years ago, and the holy *ankh* which contained a map to find it was split in half. Fat Guy explains he wants to sell the Banana to whichever country pays the most for it. Lance Sterling insults Fat Guy before agreeing to unite his half of the holy *ankh* with that of Fat Guy. However, Lance steals Fat Guy's half of the *ankh* before escaping with Slobberjob. When Fat Guy's henchmen pursue them, a woman named Nadia distracts the henchmen so they can escape. She claims Lance and Slobberjob's employers sent her to protect them, but Lance refuses her help.

Lance and Slobberjob combine the holy *ankh* pieces with a supercomputer and discover the *ankh*'s map does not point to the Banana of Bombay, only a clue to the Banana's location. They travel to Paris, meeting Nadia again after a humorous misunderstanding with a French waiter. She tells them Fat Guy and Rameet are tracking them, and after Slobberjob attempts to take on Rameet, he is thrown at an awning and discovers a map to the Banana of Bombay.

Arriving in a jungle, Lance and Slobberjob enter a temple containing the Banana of Bombay. They discover the Banana on a pillar in the middle of a pool of lava, but it is taken by Nadia. She explains she is from Moldavia, a poor country where the government has decided to invest in tourism; they need the Banana to open a fruit stand. Fat Guy and Rameet take the Banana and trap Lance, Nadia, and Slobberjob on the pillar. Rameet falls in the lava, and Slobberjob manages to get everyone off the pillar. A group of monkeys steal the Banana of Bombay from Fat Guy, but Lance and Slobberjob grab the Banana and flee the temple, pursued by Fat Guy, Nadia and the monkeys. They are cornered at a cliff, but use the Banana to make their adversaries slip and fall into a river. Rameet, who survived falling into the lava, confronts them, and they are forced to jump off the cliff.

Ending the fantasy, Garfield and Odie fall out of the refrigerator. When Jon asks Garfield if he had another fantasy, Garfield says it was his last one, only to enter another fantasy that mirrors the film *Casablanca*.

Garfield Gets A Life

This final Garfield television special was first broadcast on 8 May 1991 on CBS, and was nominated for Outstanding Animated Program at the 43rd Primetime Emmy Awards. Despite the success of *Garfield and Friends*, CBS cancelled new animated specials in 1990. Odie only appears twice in this special, which focuses mainly on Jon rather than Garfield.

On a dull Monday morning, Jon realizes how uneventful his life is and sets out to change it. He goes to various places to meet girls, but is turned down by them all. At home, Jon sees a TV ad for the Lorenzo School for the Personality Impaired and decides to attend. There, he meets a girl named Mona, and the two like each other and go to Jon's house. Garfield is worried about Jon being in a relationship and goes to tell him. Mona begins sneezing and tells Jon she is allergic to cats. Jon chooses to stay with Garfield, but he agrees to stay friends with Mona, and the two go out to dinner, followed by Garfield.

This special features noted voice actor Frank Welker, who has voiced characters in *Transformers*, *He-Man* and many other shows. In an interesting twist, Welker would go on to voice Garfield himself in *The Garfield Show* television series.

Am I Cool or What?

The music in the Garfield specials was integral to the show, with Lou Rawls and Desiree Goyette prominently featured, often as the intro music and over the end credits.

Am I Cool or What? is an album featuring songs inspired by the Garfield comic strip. It was released on 3 July 1991 by GRP Records in CD and cassette format. The genre is primarily R&B and contemporary jazz. The album features appearances by luminaries such as B.B. King and The Temptations. It peaked at number 23 on the Billboard charts for contemporary jazz albums.

In this collection of contemporary jazz/blues/smooth R&B songs themed around his life, no stone is left unturned in artists such as the Pointer Sisters, Natalie Cole and Patti LaBelle paying musical homage to Garfield. Whether commenting on his mischievous abuse of Odie, eating too much lasagna or loathing Mondays, *Am I Cool or What?* covers it all. The track listing is as follows:

1. 'Shake Your Paw' (written by Tim Camp) – The Temptations
2. 'I Love It When I'm Naughty' (Catte Adams, Will Ryan, Marc Hugenberger) – Patti LaBelle
3. 'Fat Is Where It's At' (Camp) – Carl Anderson
4. 'Long 'Bout Midnight' (Desirée Goyette, Ed Bogas) – Natalie Cole
5. 'Nine Lives' (Ryan Adams) – The Pointer Sisters
6. 'Here Comes Garfield' (Goyette, Bogas) – Lou Rawls
7. 'Next to You I'm Even Better' (Ryan Adams) – Diane Schuur
8. 'Spare Time' (David Benoit, Marcel East) – David Benoit
9. 'Up on a Fence' (Goyette, Bogas) – Desirée Goyette
10. 'Monday Morning Blues (Blues for Mr. G)' – (Patrick DeVuono, Darlene Koldenhoven) – B.B. King

'Long About Midnight', 'Here Comes Garfield' and 'Up on a Fence' were previously recorded for the soundtrack of *Here Comes Garfield* (with the former two songs appearing in the special itself). 'Shake Your Paw' and 'Monday Morning Blues' were featured in *Garfield Gets a Life*, while 'Spare Time' has the same melody as the theme song of the special.

Garfield's Judgement Day

Jim Davis wrote the script for Garfield's first feature-length theatrical cartoon while the primetime animated specials and *Garfield and Friends* were still in production. In order to pitch it, Davis used his money to fund the voice recordings, including all the signature actors reprising their roles, including Lou Rawls. Rawls and Desirée Goyette even recorded the song 'We Got It Good, And That Ain't Bad', which did not see the light of day until the TV special *Happy Birthday Garfield*. After unsuccessfully pitching it as a movie and, eventually, as a television special for several years, Davis tried writing two other feature-length scripts to studios including Walt Disney Pictures and 20th Century Fox, but still no studio showed interest. It's an example of Davis trying to push the boundaries with Garfield, and was ultimately one of his biggest failures, despite the success and awards garnered by the television specials. It is maybe why you don't see Garfield push the boundaries nowadays, but in the late 1980s Davis was becoming quite experimental and existential with Garfield. However, at the time, *Garfield and Friends* had just started on television, and a Garfield film was maybe a step too far, especially with this one's darker tones. Garfield would have to wait a little longer until he got to the big screen, and in the meantime would go through quite a transformation, taking him out of the cartoon world, turning him computer-animated and putting him into the real world. It would have been interesting to see a film with the title *Judgement Day*, which would probably have been released before James Cameron's 1991 *Terminator* sequel *T2: Judgement Day*.

Unfortunately, *Garfield's Judgement Day* was not meant to be as an animated film, but lives on as one of Garfield's most curious adventures in literature.

Chapter 11

Garfield and Friends

In the mid-1990s, Garfield was brought to a new generation with the creation of *Garfield and Friends*. With TV specials on CBS having done tremendously well, a new animated show was developed by CBS and Davis. The show ran on CBS on Saturday mornings from 17 September 1988 to 10 December 1994, with reruns airing until 7 October 1995. Produced by Film Roman, in association with United Feature Syndicate and Paws, Inc., seven seasons of the series were produced. Inspired by the traditional format of animated cartoons like *Looney Tunes* and *Popeye*, *Garfield and Friends* featured several different episodes within one thirty-minute or hour-long slot. Garfield went up against fellow Saturday morning cartoons that were inspired by Japanese cartoon conventions, such as *Transformers*, whose episodes were a story which took up the entire thirty minutes.

The series was greatly influenced by the comic strips, with episodes from the first series relying on plenty of gags from them. There were also animated segments from Davis' *U.S. Acres*, retitled *Orson's Farm* for viewers outside the United States (taking the name of their main character, Orson Pig). Although Davis stopped producing new strips of *U.S. Acres/Orson's Farm* seven months after *Garfield and Friends* debuted, the characters continued to appear until the series ceased production.

Unlike the comic strip, where characters could go months without being seen, *Garfield and Friends* introduced us to an ensemble of Garfield characters, all of whom played pivotal roles in the series. Instead of being background characters, the likes of Odie, Dr Liz and Nermal all became regular supporting characters, featuring in multiple episodes throughout the course of the series.

Characters

Garfield (voiced by Lorenzo Music): The series continues to portray Garfield as a fat, lazy, sarcastic orange tabby cat, who wants nothing more out of life than to eat, drink coffee and sleep. He continues to announce his love for consuming lasagne, his enjoyment of tormenting Odie and trying to mail Nermal to Abu Dhabi. He makes a handful of appearances in *U.S. Acres*, in the segments 'Mystery Guest', 'Fast Food', 'Quack to the Future' and 'The Thing In the Box', although he is more often seen in the form of various pieces of Garfield-themed merchandise the *U.S. Acres* characters appear to own. Deep down, Garfield loves Jon and Odie. Garfield does not speak out loud, but his thoughts are heard by everyone. This is revealed in one episode to be via the use of a special microphone which amplifies the thoughts of animals apart from Odie.

'Lorenzo Music had that gift of being able to throw a line away while doing it with great comedic timing. It captured Garfield's attitude so perfectly that I found myself writing the dialogue for Lorenzo rather than the cat. I still hear Lorenzo's voice when I write for Garfield,' Davis said of Lorenzo, who became the iconic voice of Garfield thanks to his role. 'He had a way of throwing a line away and not really caring about it. Everything was said with such comedic timing and made you laugh. That's very rare. Especially back in the day when comedians were pretty much over the top, pretty much stand-up kind of timing and stuff like that. He was really a departure, and he captured the spirit of Garfield so perfectly.'

Lorenzo Music's low-key drawl as Garfield was utterly fantastic and one of the main reasons why the show was so successful. In perfect symmetry, Lorenzo Music also provided the voice of Peter Venkman in *The Real Ghostbusters* cartoon of the 1980s, while playing Peter Venkman in the original *Ghostbusters* film was Bill Murray, who voiced Garfield in 2004's *Garfield: The Movie*.

Jon Arbuckle (Thom Huge): Jon is portrayed as a bachelor cartoonist who has no luck with women and a somewhat nerdy demeanour. He is often annoyed by Garfield's antics, and whenever Garfield gets in trouble, Jon punishes him by taking away his lasagne, not letting him watch television or taking him to the vet. He tries to convince Garfield to do the right thing whenever he gets into trouble. Jon occasionally forces Garfield to lose weight and catch mice, which is always unsuccessful due to Garfield not wanting to eat mice and his friendship with one such mouse named Floyd.

Thom Huge had previously voiced characters, including Jon himself in various Garfield TV specials, starting with *Garfield on the Town*. Thom also voiced Binky The Clown.

Odie (Gregg Berger): The yellow Beagle is Garfield's sometimes best friend, sometimes enemy. He used to belong to Jon's former roommate Lyman (a character from the earliest comic strips who is absent from the show). A running gag has Garfield kicking him off a kitchen table. Though he does not seem all that intelligent, Odie is actually more cunning and smart than he sometimes lets on. Odie is the only animal character who does not communicate with any form of dialogue in *Garfield and Friends*, instead communicating with body language, barking and other dog sound effects, although Garfield is able to understand what he is saying.

Gregg Berger is a voice actor most famous for voicing Grimlock in *The Transformers* cartoon. He was a mainstay in animation during the 1980s and 1990s. His acting credits include *Gargoyles*, *Aaah!!! Real Monsters*, *G.I. Joe*, *Rugrats* and additional voices on *The Simpsons*. During the 2000s, he worked as a video game voice actor, with roles in 'Viewtiful Joe', 'Call Of Duty', 'Dishonoured', 'Dead Rising' and various 'Final Fantasy' games.

Nermal (Desirée Goyette): Garfield is insanely jealous of the cute grey tabby kitten, the self-proclaimed 'World's Cutest Kitty Cat'. Nermal seems kind and playful, although this upbeat positivity annoys Garfield. Nermal is often caught bragging about how much cuter and more fun he is. Garfield often attempts (usually unsuccessfully) to mail him to Abu Dhabi as a result. Though officially considered a male, Nermal's feminine preoccupation with being cute, and the fact that a woman provides a soft, childlike voice, meant the character was often mistaken for a female cat: indeed, in the first two seasons, the Spanish version of the show features Nermal as a female kitten named Thelma.

Binky the Clown (Thom Huge): The very loud, obnoxious and annoying clown appeared several times in the comic strip before becoming a fairly regular character on *Garfield and Friends*. Within the series, Binky has his own TV show that Garfield and Odie try to avoid watching, though it seems Binky's show can magically appear. Binky sometimes has his own short segment on the series, 'Screaming with Binky', that runs at the midway point of an hour-long episode, but most of these segments were removed in syndication. 'Screaming with Binky' segments were only aired in seasons 2 and 3 (1989–91) of the show, and some were re-aired for a month after eight weeks of season 4 and 5 episodes (November 1991–September 1993). Binky's catchphrase is 'Hey, kids!', with the vowels prolonged; to Garfield, he yells 'Hey, cat!', with an extended 'e'. After being a recurring character for the first three seasons, Binky appeared only sporadically. He returned in the season 7 episode 'The Feline Philosopher', his last episode in the show.

Herman Post (Gregg Berger): Herman is a mailman who loves delivering the mail, despite being a frequent victim of Garfield's booby traps. As with Binky, he rarely appears after season 3.

Dr Elizabeth 'Liz' Wilson (Julie Payne): Garfield and Odie's sarcastic vet is Jon's main love interest. She occasionally dates him, but these outings always end in disaster, often due to Garfield's antics. She only appears in the show's first two seasons, except for one appearance in the season 4 episode 'Frankenstein Feline', Davis perhaps feeling that the love interest angle in the television show wasn't as interesting as in the comic strip.

Floyd (Gregg Berger): Garfield's mouse friend takes the place of his mouse friend Squeak from the comic strip. Floyd originally appears as an antagonist in the season 1 episode 'Good Mousekeeping', when he and his fellow mice stay at Jon's house after discovering that Garfield does not eat mice, but they are eventually driven out of the house. He becomes friends with Garfield in his second appearance, the season 1 episode 'Identity Crisis'. He appears in every season of the show, but only in a handful of episodes in each. He has a friend named Tyrone in the season 3 episode 'Rodent Rampage' and a wife named April in season 6's 'The Floyd Story'.

Pooky: Garfield's teddy bear and sleeping companion, of whom Jon is jealous, does not speak. Found in a drawer, he is Garfield's only toy. Garfield adopts his alter ego 'The Caped Avenger' after temporarily losing Pooky.

The quality of *Garfield and Friends* compared with other 1980s animated television series has been considered by animation historian Jerry Beck to 'foreshadow the higher quality [animation] boom coming in the next decade'. Garfield was perhaps a major inspiration for the resurgence of animal characters in the 1990s and the segmented style of cartoons like *Animaniacs*, *Tiny Toons* and Nickelodeon shows such as *Angry Beavers*, *Rocko's Modern Life* and *Cat Dog*.

Who can forget the incredible theme song of *Garfield and Friends*, 'Friends Are There'? The iconic theme featured the *U.S. Acres* gang as well as Garfield in a back-and-forth for screen supremacy. It was the first time Garfield had mixed with the *U.S. Acres* characters. Each episode opened with Gary Owens, one of the most recognizable American DJs of the late twentieth century, introducing the show by saying, 'Ladies and gentlemen, Garfield and Friends!'. The first five seasons had Garfield tap dancing on a fence, turning on a record player for the animated introduction, but with season 6 the animation changed and it opened with a full concert hall.

While many people are familiar with the first theme song, *Garfield and Friends* actually had two more distinctive themes over its seven-season run. A more upbeat and lively song, 'We're Ready To Party', first appeared in episode 9 of the third season and was used until the end of season 6. This time, Garfield sang the song along with the rest of the cast, and the intro consisted of clips from previous episodes of the series. This intro was also used for the syndicated rerun package, but all incidental music from the first two seasons' worth of episodes was left intact. It was not until the DVD releases that the intros from those seasons were seen in their entirety again.

In the seventh and final season of *Garfield and Friends*, an upbeat rap-based theme song was used, sung by J.R. Johnston, which had a bass line similar to that of the *Seinfeld* theme. This theme is not included on the DVDs (on the DVD set and in all international versions, the rap theme is replaced with 'We're Ready To Party'), nor did it make its way onto the rerun package of *Garfield and Friends*, which is a shame as it's a fun song.

The close of each version of the theme brought out the show's title screen, where Booker, from *U.S. Acres*, writes 'and friends' in pencil below Garfield's name. Garfield would then appear atop the title and offer a joke to open the show. Regular segments featured both Garfield and *U.S. Acres*, the latter retitled *Orson's Farm* for foreign syndication as well as the DVD releases as it was felt that *U.S. Acres* wouldn't really lend itself to the foreign market.

In total, 242 Garfield segments and 121 *U.S. Acres* segments were produced. There were two 'Garfield' segments on each show, two 'quickie' shorts based on Sunday comic strips, and in between was a *U.S. Acres* segment.

A total of 121 half-hour shows were produced, and all have been released on five DVD sets by 20th Century Fox Home Entertainment; 9 Story Media Group is remastering the series for High-Definition. The intro was reanimated in Flash and some animation frames are missing.

The first season aired in a half-hour format. In the second season, it switched to an hour-length format, showing two episodes each week. In the show's last season, the second half-hour of the show featured either an episode from the previous season or one of the Garfield TV specials.

Garfield and Friends had already far outlasted most other animated series by the time it reached its seventh season in 1994. Although Garfield was still doing well in the ratings, the Saturday morning cartoon genre had begun a decline by this point, and CBS began to cut its cartoon budget, despite other cartoons being successful on weekdays. Unwilling to continue producing the show under the reduced budget, producers brought the series to an end in 1994.

The series has been acquired by Viacom, as part of the company's purchase of the franchise. As of early 2020, *Garfield and Friends* was not on any streaming platforms, despite *The Garfield Show* being on Netflix.

U.S. Acres (Orson's Farm)

U.S. Acres (known as Orson's Farm outside the United States, and as Orson's Place in Canada) was a comic strip that originally ran from 1986–89, created by Jim Davis himself. U.S. Acres was Davis' attempt to branch out and away from Garfield, breathing life into a small farm, with farmyard animals, inspired again by his childhood in rural Indiana.

'I did it just to do something for very young readers and to do something big. I grew up on a farm, big and bright, and at that time, we had a very successful run with our primetime specials,' Davis said, in reference to his Garfield specials.

U.S. Acres was launched on 3 March 1986 by United Feature Syndicate in a then-unprecedented 505 newspapers. Brett Koth, who was an assistant to Davis on the Garfield strip at that time and much like Davis had been an assistant to T.K. Ryan, was given co-creator's credit on the new strip, on which he signed his name along with Davis. It was an unprecedented move for Davis to share the credit on the strip, giving his assistant a co-creator credit. The strip was centred on a group of barnyard animals, the main character being Orson, a small pig who had been taken from his mother shortly after being born.

Davis recalls: 'CBS wanted us to do Saturday morning. I said, "Half an hour is a lot of time with just one cat." I think every Saturday, we'd wear them out, plus it's a lot of material. However, if you put *U.S. Acres* in there, we could hop back and forth at least, and break up the monotony.'

At the peak of the comic strip's popularity, there were children's books, plush animals (particularly of the characters Roy, Booker, Sheldon and Orson) and posters of the main characters. Its animated adaptation was included in the *Garfield and Friends* show, and continued to be for several years after the strip ended, which was even lamp shaded in one of the final strips. The final U.S. Acres daily strip was printed on 15 April 1989, while the final Sunday one appeared on 7 May that year. Most papers only ran the Sunday strip, usually on the same page as Garfield.

The strip was relaunched as an online webcomic on 1 October 2010. The relaunch was announced the day before in a question-and-answer column in *USA Today*. Later, in celebration of U.S. Acres' twenty-fourth anniversary, the strips prior to 1 August 1986 were released on Garfield.com.

The U.S. Acres comic strip was included on the Go Comics website from 3 March 2012, the twenty-sixth anniversary of its original debut. On 7 August 2016, a Garfield comic strip showed the U.S. Acres gang (*sans* Bo and Blue) in its logo box, featuring Garfield eating a bag of chicken feed.

Davis said of U.S. Acres:

'I did it for the young readers. In fact, the strip only ran, I think, for three years. It started with a lot of papers, but I was sitting across from the editor of the *Boston Globe*, and he said he didn't think he was going to be keeping U.S. Acres. I said, "Why not? It's for young readers." He says, "Kids don't buy our advertising." And that was the mentality. We were winning comics polls with young readers.'

But with the media landscape changing, it was the juggernaut that is Garfield which managed to outlast the printed newspapers and move into the next generation on the internet.

U.S. Acres being aimed primarily at children was something that Davis was proud of, and was something that he would take more of an interest in in later years with Garfield educational programmes for children.

Davis continued:

'At any rate, circulation was down; Garfield was taking as much, or more time, and we just made a really tough decision. We were still in several hundred papers, but I opted to end the [U.S. Acres] series just because of all this stuff going on. I didn't want to do a second-rate job on Garfield, so I just had to end it, but I loved doing it. The shows still run today in syndication. People still know the characters. We had more fun with Wade the Duck, [a] panaphobe, [who was] afraid of everything.'

In August 2019, much like Garfield, the rights to U.S. Acres were sold to Viacom as part of its acquisition of Paws, Inc. With a new Garfield show rumoured to be in development at Nickelodeon, the future is strong for the Garfield brand.

For many, *Garfield and Friends* is the perfect encapsulation of Garfield the character. It is perhaps down to nostalgia, but the series remains a standout for newcomers and fans alike. The mix of *Garfield* and *U.S Acres*, along with the length of the story, make them bite-sized snapshots of Garfield. Many believe that Lorenzo Music's voice in the shows is the perfect depiction of Garfield.

Notable and Fan Favourite Episodes

Peace & Quiet

Garfield has watched TV all night after Jon leaves the set on, so the tired cat tries to take a long nap while Jon and Odie go out to run errands. Unfortunately for Garfield, Binky the Clown shows up at the door to deliver a special birthday greeting to 'Mrs Edna Fogerty' and will not leave until he completes his quest.

This may be the first episode of the show's first series, but it is a very funny one. You get the predictable story of somebody trying to keep someone else from their slumber; it's a plot straight out of a Tex Avery or Bugs Bunny cartoon, only this time it's Garfield trying to keep Binky the Clown out of the house. But at the same time, the jokes get the job done by making you laugh regardless of how predictable the outcome of the episode becomes. It sets up the tension nicely between Garfield and his least favourite clown.

Basket Brawl

This episode is set at a basketball game that mice attend, with Jon, Odie and Nermal attempting to pack a picnic lunch without Garfield devouring all the food, which proves troublesome.

What makes this episode such a great one is how it's setup: it's like you're watching an NBA basketball game on TV, right down to Chick Hearn – then of CBS Sports' NBA coverage – voicing one of the mice announcing the game. There's even a Jack Nicholson mouse, the Hollywood star being famous for attending L.A. Lakers games. Episodes like this are evidence of the unique and inventive way Davis and the production staff created these stories.

The Multiple Choice Cartoon

Garfield gives the audience a unique episode where they can make choices on what happens in the cartoon. This is when the show was at its best, with these unusual, off-the-cuff episodes with unique premises. The episode does a good job of having different outcomes to a particular scene, all of which would have made for interesting outcomes, and the jokes work perfectly well. However, one downside is that all of the clips they picked are the letter 'C'; I understand this was made for kids, but you could at least vary it a bit with the choices. Other than that, it is a really good episode.

The Binky Show
It is strange to think that the annoying clown Binky keeps appearing in the best of episodes, but his antagonistic nature works so well when he has Garfield as his foil. When Jon's birthday arrives, Garfield panics as he has no money to get Jon anything. To win Jon a present, Garfield goes on a game show titled 'Name That Fish', hosted by Binky the Clown. The concept is simple, but gets more and more ridiculous as the episode continues, right down to an obvious but still funny twist at the conclusion, and it ends up being one of the most entertaining episodes of *Garfield and Friends*.

Video Airlines
Garfield, Jon and Odie want to watch a movie, but the only one on TV is *Kung Fu Creatures on the Rampage 2*, which none of them are interested in. They seek out alternative ways to watch a movie, unaware of the prevalence of *Kung Fu Creatures on the Rampage 2*. The concept is that every single movie they end up watching is the same one throughout the course of the episode. This premise leads to plenty of comedy and a really funny pay-off.

Mini-Mall Matters
Garfield hosts a factual and educational show about mini-malls, how they are grown, maintained and their features. Another reason why the *Garfield and Friends* show worked so well was how serious they took such ridiculous concepts, in this case mini-malls, including how they are just planted in the ground like a garden. Arguably, Garfield isn't known for satire, but in this episode it really works.

The Cartoon Cat Conspiracy
Garfield reveals the injustice that cartoon cats must suffer, so he decides to make his own animated feature where he gets his own way. What makes this episode work is, again, the satirical element and Garfield breaking the 'fourth wall'. This episode lampoons the classic Hanna-Barbera and Tex Avery style animation in the opening scene, while also making fun of

the cartoon clichés and tropes in the types of cartoons Garfield is talking about. Much like *The Simpsons* with Fox, they poke fun at the network they are on, CBS.

The Big Talker

Garfield is furious with Joe Palaver, a loudmouth television host who hates cats and says they have no use whatsoever. After finding out that Palaver is superstitious, Garfield carries out revenge.

This was before Jerry Springer, before Maury Povich, before Fox News, and essentially before any of those 'loud-mouthed trash-talking' TV personalities were so ubiquitous. This was during the time when talk show host Morton Downey Jr was seen as the biggest trash-talker on TV, and essentially it is he who is being parodied here. The story itself is about as predictable as you can get, but the jokes definitely carry through.

Heatwave Holiday

During an especially hot summer day, Garfield decides to think about colder climates. This eventually develops into a trend throughout the city of decorating for Christmas in the middle of July. Everyone is thrilled to celebrate Christmas a little early.

The story itself starts off simply, but the episode is turned on its head with a really solid twist, leading to lots of clever and funny little jokes about how one small thing can make so many people automatically think it's Christmas. It's a very silly concept, but because Garfield takes it to the limit, it winds up being one of the finest episodes.

Mistakes Will Happen

In response to letters about errors on the show, Garfield tries to convince viewers that his show doesn't have any mistakes. He and Odie then watch a cartoon which has a vast number of mistakes.

This is when *Garfield & Friends* was at its best. Like with 'The Cartoon Cat Conspiracy', this episode satirizes all different aspects of animation. It highlights how you will see lots of mistakes in many of Garfield's contemporary cartoons: from random things popping out of nowhere to pointless cameos, wrong animation loops, lines of dialogue not matching up to what's on screen, Jon constantly getting characters' names wrong – including his own – and different voice actors playing the characters.

There's even a section where Garfield fluffs a line and they keep in the voice of the voice director.

This episode essentially parodies how cartoons like *Teenage Mutant Ninja Turtles*, many of the Filmation animations and even Warner Bros. cartoons would have these obvious animation errors, but the story just goes along as scheduled with the characters not acknowledging the mistakes. Keep in mind, this episode aired in 1990, right around the time of *Tiny Toon Adventures* but three years before *Animaniacs* satirized the animated cartoon, so this is one of the many reasons why the show was so clever and ahead of its time in terms of satirical comedy.

'Mistakes Will Happen' perfectly sums up what made *Garfield and Friends* such a great show and is one of the most unique and inventive episodes. *Garfield and Friends* managed to slip satire into Garfield, breathing life into the characters and their world, whereas the newspaper strip didn't really do that.

The Garfield Show

The Garfield Show was a French-American CGI animated television series, created by Jim Davis and produced by Dargaud Media, along with Paws, Inc. It focused on a new series of adventures for the characters of Garfield, Odie and Jon, alongside staple characters from the strip and a number of unique additions for the programme. This was a step away from *Garfield and Friends* in terms of content, look and feel. Whereas *Garfield and Friends* was traditional animation, *The Garfield Show* was a CGI 3D rendered show and was aimed at slightly younger children. Both Davis and producer Mark Evanier, who previously wrote episodes for the 1988 animated series of *Garfield and Friends*, co-wrote stories for the show, with the cast including Frank Welker, Wally Wingert, Julie Payne, Jason Marsden and Gregg Berger.

The blurb for the show, which summed it up nicely, was, 'Everyone's favourite fat cat Garfield returns to television in this new CG animated cartoon. To celebrate his 30th anniversary, every one of your favourite characters return too. Jon, Odie, Arlene, Nermal and more return in the new series as well.'

The series premiered on 22 December 2008 in France and 2 November 2009 in the United States. It ran for five seasons, with 109 episodes, its last episode airing in America on 24 October 2016. Evanier stated shortly afterwards that the show was on hiatus.

The show features a loose continuity and is set in a different universe to *Garfield and Friends*, which is occasionally referenced. Unlike the previous show, Liz is now considered a main character and has an official relationship with Jon to reflect their status in the comic strip. *The Garfield Show* also re-establishes Arlene as Garfield's potential love interest, as in the comic strip, replacing Penelope from the previous show (despite being touted as a main character, her actual role in the series is relatively minor). In addition, unlike the previous series and animated specials, where Garfield thought instead of speaking his dialogue, Garfield is now a fully fledged talking character.

The Garfield Show also features many new characters as part of the regular cast, such as Vito, an Italian chef whose cooking Garfield enjoys, and Squeak, Garfield's mouse friend who lives in Jon's house (replacing Floyd from the previous show). Like *Garfield and Friends*, *The Garfield Show* had different segments, but the *U.S. Acres* cast does not appear. Many of the original crew members would return to work on *The Garfield Show*, including voice actors and production staff.

English-language episodes started airing on Boomerang UK on 5 May 2009, and later on Pop and Nicktoons UK. English-language episodes also started airing on Boomerang (Middle East and Africa) and Boomerang (Central and Eastern Europe) on 7 November 2009, while it aired on YTV in Canada from 13 September 2009 to 30 December 2011. In the United States, it aired on the Cartoon Network from 2 November 2009 to 30 May 2014. It also aired on Boomerang from 4 February 2013 to 30 December 2016.

Notable Episode

Orange and Black (which originally aired in France under the title 'Catzilla') is a Halloween special of *The Garfield Show*.

It is Halloween night and Garfield has already eaten all of the candy which was intended for trick-or-treaters, leaving only some stale taffy candy which was left over from last year's Halloween. In order to get some more candy, Garfield decides to go trick-or-treating himself (very similar to *Garfield's Halloween Adventure*). He has difficulty choosing a costume, but reasons that the scarier the costume, the more candy the trick-or-treater will receive. Turning on the TV in search of inspiration, he sees a news report about a new arrival at the zoo, Catzilla, a rare descendant of the prehistoric sabre-toothed tiger and the scariest animal to be seen at the zoo for a long time. Garfield decides that Catzilla would make the perfect costume for him. He paints black stripes on his front, to match those on his back, takes some tusks from a toy walrus to complete his disguise and practices looking ferocious in front of the mirror.

As Garfield leaves the house, Jon and Odie hear another news report. It says that Catzilla has just escaped from the zoo and that residents are warned to be on the lookout for the dangerous creature. Garfield is unaware of this.

At each house that he goes to, Garfield is mistaken for the real Catzilla. All the people who see him are so scared that they drop their entire bowl of candy in fright, each bowl landing in Garfield's bag. He is delighted to receive twenty-three bowls of candy at twenty-three houses, but is disappointed that his haul does not include any peanut brittle. Garfield's fun ends abruptly when the police arrive, believing him to be Catzilla and wanting to take him back to the zoo. Garfield runs home, but when Jon sees him outside, he calls the police to tell them Catzilla is outside his house. As Garfield is taken away to the zoo, the real Catzilla sneaks into Jon's house.

At the zoo, Garfield is placed in Catzilla's cage. He tries to escape, before realizing that he only has to remove the toy walrus tusks to show that he isn't Catzilla. When a zookeeper sees that the animal in the cage is just an overweight house cat, he has no choice but to let Garfield go.

Garfield arrives home just as Catzilla is about to attack Jon and Odie. Realizing that giving him something to eat would keep Catzilla occupied for a while, Garfield feeds him last year's stale taffy. Catzilla has great difficulty chewing the old candy, which glues his teeth together so he cannot bite anyone. Soon afterwards, the police arrive and Catzilla is returned to the zoo.

At the end of the episode, Jon and Garfield are visiting the zoo. The zookeeper who had earlier freed Garfield tells them that it is Catzilla's feeding time and that he is about to be fed large quantities of steak, salmon, roast beef, lasagne and peanut brittle. Hearing this, Garfield slips into Catzilla's cage and joins him for his meal.

Garfield Originals

Garfield Originals is a 2019–20 2D French animated series created by Jim Davis and Philippe Vidal. The series was developed with France's Dargaud Media and Ellipsanime and was the third animated series based on the comic strip, following *Garfield and Friends* and *The Garfield Show*. It is similar to the 'Garfield Quickies', which appeared in *Garfield and Friends*, and the 'Garfield Shorts', a series of short films containing gags. It was first showcased on Dargaud Media and Mediatoon Distribution's website, then announced on the official Garfield website. Dargaud Media and Paws, Inc. had previously collaborated on *The Garfield Show*, and with this ambitious new project they created 120 short films, each just thirty seconds long. Each episode contains five short films. Twelve short films were available on the France TV website in 2020, although they could only be viewed in France.

Madlab Animations, originally created by Ankama Animations and Ellipsanime Productions, was the animation studio for the show. *Garfield Originals* was acquired by Viacom as part of the company's purchase of the Garfield franchise, joining a group of children's franchises at Nickelodeon that included the brand-defining *SpongeBob SquarePants*, *Paw Patrol* and *Teenage Mutant Ninja Turtles*. It will be interesting to see how Garfield will fit into the new landscape of children's television. With the acquisition of Garfield in such a high-profile way and for such a huge sum of money, it could well turn out to be the crown jewel in Nickelodeon programming.

Chapter 12

Video Games

A Week Of Garfield

'Week of Garfield' is a 1989 Famicom title in which Garfield is the main character. It was a Japan-only release. A prototype surfaced online on 16 March 2019, with emulators making fans able to play it. 'A Week of Garfield' takes place over seven days, naturally, with each level representing a different day of the week. We will assume that Garfield finds the Monday level the hardest!

Each level has different power-ups that can be found by moving over them; these can give Garfield increased health or more ammunition for his collection of four weapons. Garfield can fight his enemies using four different weapons: kicks, a bone that flies straight forward, a bomb that splits into four, and three spread-out bullets. If a weapon's ammunition runs out, Garfield will not be able to use it until he acquires more. The only attack that does not require ammunition is the basic kick. Levels are divided into multiple segments, and Garfield must find a key at the end of each segment. Later in the game, the keys are guarded by an alley cat who attacks Garfield. Each level has a time limit within it, inspired by games with speed running in mind like 'Super Mario World of Sonic The Hedgehog'. When a level is completed, Jon appears and says something, leading to the start of the next level.

Garfield Labyrinth

The European game 'Garfield Labyrinth', known in the United States as 'The Real Ghostbusters' and in Japan as 'Mickey Mouse IV: Mahō no Labyrinth', is a 1993 action-puzzle video game developed by Kemco and published in Japan and Europe by Kotobuki Systems and in North America by Activision.

The European version is based on Jim Davis' Garfield comic strips and the animated series *Garfield and Friends*, while the Japanese version is based on Walt Disney's Mickey Mouse and is part of the Mickey Mouse side of Kemco's Crazy Castle series. The North American version is based on the animated series *The Real Ghostbusters* and contains ten more stages than the previous incarnations.

The game is a direct lift of 'P.P. Hammer and his Pneumatic Weapon', featuring simplified sprites and near-identical level designs. According to the developer of 'P.P. Hammer', the port is entirely unauthorized.

Depending on which version is played, the player controls either Garfield, Mickey Mouse or Peter Venkman. The game emphasizes puzzle-solving in a dungeon-like atmosphere. The player has to collect stars, which open the door to the next level. In the North American version, the player has a proton gun instead of a pneumatic hammer, but it's only effective on blocks at the character's feet, not on the ghosts, which must be destroyed with bombs. If the player character loses all his health (by touching damaging things like ghosts, flames and reforming blocks), or the 999-second timer winds down to zero, he loses a life.

The player is rewarded with a twelve-digit password after successful completion of a level, which enables them to start at the end of that level next time they play. An inventory screen is present in the Japanese version of the game.

The storyline features the two main characters (depending on the version) trying to cross a bridge. When the main character falls from the bridge, he tries to shout at the secondary character for help. All three versions of the game have a variation on the pneumatic hammer, which enhances the puzzle-solving element of the game. Venkman, however, lacks a non-player character companion (from the other Ghostbusters) in the North American version of the game and simply mutters to himself prior to falling through the broken bridge.

This is probably one of the strangest video games in Garfield's history.

Garfield: A Tail Of Two Kitties

'Garfield: A Tail of Two Kitties' is a series of 3D action adventure games based on the film of the same name, and versions were released for PC, Playstation 2 and Nintendo DS. You play as Garfield in all versions; however, you can switch characters in the PlayStation 2 and Windows versions (to Christophe and Claudius). The gameplay loosely follows the plot of the movie.

In the Nintendo DS version, Garfield must travel all through England to get to the castle in time for dinner. Along the way, you may collect various food items, such as hero sandwiches, burgers and soft drinks. These are not important to the game, but add interest. The game consists of twenty-three levels (level one being an introduction of sorts), and there is a time attack mode for some levels.

The game starts with a quick tutorial. Then the real game starts in the garden. You must help Garfield defeat boss Dargis by completing missions in four areas of the castle. In the Nintendo DS version, the prince invites Garfield to a lasagne dinner at his castle.

'Garfield: A Tail of Two Kitties' received moderate reviews. GameRankings and Metacritic gave it a score of 71.5 per cent and seventy-two out of 100 for the PC version, and 63.35 per cent and fifty-nine out of 100 for the DS version, which is good for a Garfield game as many such games are criticized for being lazy or mere cash-ins.

Garfield: Big Fat Hairy Deal

'Garfield: Big Fat Hairy Deal' (they really know how to name their games!) is a 1987 computer game for the Atari ST, ZX Spectrum, Commodore 64, Amstrad CPC and Amiga. The plot involves Arlene being captured by Animal Control and put in the city pound, and it is up to Garfield to save her.

In this side scrolling adventure, Garfield is able to walk, kick, crawl and jump. He can pick up items, walk around the house, enter passages, go into the sewer and walk around the neighbourhood. Garfield has a sleep meter and a hunger meter. If Garfield's hunger meter gets too low, he will shout 'SNACK ATTACK!' and eat the item he is holding, which fills up the meter. The sleep meter can be refilled by staying still. If Garfield's sleep meter gets too low, or Garfield's hunger meter is empty without him holding anything, the game ends.

Garfield starts his quest in Jon's house, and has to venture through streets, dark alleys, convalescent homes and sewers to find Arlene. Various objects are littered along the way, and Garfield meets characters including Odie, Nermal and giant rats that can help or hinder his quest.

In some versions of this game, the background graphics are only in black and white, but the sprites show a little colour. In other versions (the Commodore 64 version) the graphics are all full colour.

In a nice touch, posters with Binky the Clown and the phrases 'I WANT YOU' and 'JOIN THE CIRCUS' – similar to the 15 September 1986 comic strip – are occasionally seen on building walls around the city.

Garfield: Caught in the Act

'Garfield: Caught in the Act' is a platform game by Sega. It was originally released in 1995 for the Sega Genesis/Mega Drive, but later had an 8-bit version released for the Sega Game Gear and the 16-bit version ported to PC. Each platform had notable differences. It was inspired by games like Disney's 'Aladdin' and 'The Lion King', both of which had sold huge numbers on Sega and for Nintendo. 'Garfield: Caught in the Act' arrived in 1995, just as the Sega Genesis was nearing the end of its lifespan.

'I've known [Sega of America president] Tom Kalinske ... for 15 years,' Garfield creator Davis said when speaking of the genesis of the game. 'We always thought [a Garfield video game] would be a good idea, but neither of us was ready. I didn't have the time to devote to it because of other projects. Two years ago Tom felt the time was right, so we started.'

'Caught in the Act' is certainly one of Garfield's most expansive and beautiful games, though the controls have been labelled as clunky.

In the game, while Garfield is watching television, Odie scares him and he ends up falling on the TV, breaking it. The two quickly try to reassemble it before Jon comes home and catches them. They end up with a crudely made television, leaving out a couple of spare parts. As Garfield throws away the spare pieces, they become an electronic monster known as Glitch, who transports Garfield into the TV. Garfield must travel through various films in order to defeat the monster and make his way back home.

The game is a platformer, with Garfield being able to attack enemies up close or throw objects at them (the close-range weapons and the objects thrown change between each level). There are also two special stages; one which resembles a 'Whac-A-Mole' game and another in which Garfield flies through a tunnel, trying to grab Pookys for an extra life.

All the sprites and hand-drawn animation in 'Garfield: Caught in the Act' were created by Davis and the artists at Paws, Inc., while Sega interActive transposed the sketches lent by the studio into pixel art graphics, with Michael Fernie, one of the programmers involved in the game's development, stating that the person who did the process was a subcontractor. The game drew inspiration from Davis' 1984 book *Garfield: His 9 Lives*. Davis noted that the concept for his book allowed them to portray Garfield as more 'kinetic' than his usual newspaper strip character, facilitating the book's adaptation into an hour-long TV special, and reasoned that a similar premise would allow a more effective translation of Garfield into the video game medium. Davis also stated he was responsible for creating both the cover art and the introduction sequence.

Interesting titbits and power-ups in the game include hamburgers and pizza, which revive Garfield's health. Garfield can find cups of coffee (named Java in the manual), which give him invincibility. Pooky, Garfield's beloved teddy bear, also makes appearances, and acts like a checkpoint, to which Garfield will return if he loses a life. If you find a mallet, you unlock the 'whack-a-mole' bonus round, while finding one of the Garfield heads earns an extra life.

Levels in the original Genesis game included Count Slobula's Castle, which is a Castlevania-inspired level with ghouls and skeletons; Revenge of Orangebeard, which includes poisonous piranhas and mischievous monkeys in a level set on the high seas (this level is slightly reminiscent of 'Donkey Kong'); Cave Cat 3,000,000 BC, set in an underground cave, which reminds players of those in 'Super Mario World'; Catsablanca, where you must dodge belligerent bulldogs and nasty neighbours; and The Curse of Cleofatra, an Egyptian-style level, slightly inspired by 'Prince Of Persia'. In the final level, called Season Finale, in Television Wasteland, players must defeat the evil glitch.

'Garfield: The Lost Levels' is a lost version of 'Garfield: Caught in the Act' that supposedly included levels cut from the original game. Magazines and merchandise have proven that 16-bit versions of the cut levels existed, as well as the fact that several people have testified to its existence, though the cartridge and ROM's current whereabouts are unknown.

In December 1994, Sega opened the Sega Channel, a pay-to-play service on the Genesis in which subscribers could access and download Genesis games, play demos and access 'cheats' through an adapter. The line-up of games used to change bi-weekly to monthly, in order to give subscribers a more varied experience. Each game was put into a specific category, with the Test Drives having upcoming and newly released titles.

Though some American Sega Channel schedules are not available, 'The Lost Levels' has three known appearances on the service: 1 February 1996 in the Test Drives, 25 April 1997 in the Family Room and 15 August 1997 in the Family Room.

As the game first appeared in the Test Drives category, that has been accepted as its first public appearance. Similarly to the American Sega Channel schedules, a couple of UK ones are missing and only one appearance of 'The Lost Levels' is known of on 1 August 1997 in the Family Room.

The internet's oldest mention of 'The Lost Levels' dates back to 4 February 1996, when a cable company owner by the name of David Madden announced the Sega Channel listings for the month.

The following levels were removed from the Genesis version of the game. Possible reasons for their removal include not being fun or distinct enough, lack of time or budget, programming difficulties and memory limitations of the Genesis hardware.

Bonehead the Barbarian and Slobbin Hood were featured only in the Game Gear version of the game, while an Alien Landscape appeared on a PC game and, thanks to a t-shirt used as merchandise for the game, we know that a level set in Ancient Rome was possibly planned too.

Catsablanca Train Sequence

Featured on no other platforms, there was apparently a train segment in the Catsablanca level that was supposed to be featured on the Sega Genesis version, but was ultimately cut. It is assumed that it was featured on 'The Lost Levels'. A similar sequence, involving cars instead of a train, was used for the Game Gear version of Catsablanca.

Although it was inspired by many fantastic games, 'Garfield: Caught in the Act' floundered slightly in reviews. While many reviewers praised the beautiful visuals and settings – so far removed from what we would see in a Garfield strip or even in *Garfield and Friends* – most focused on the sluggish movements and slow gameplay. *Sega Saturn Magazine* said, 'Once you've overcome the novelty of eliciting any movement from the world's most notorious sleep junkie, you're left with a fairly unoriginal platformer.' *Game Pro* noted that 'colorful backgrounds and big sprites will charm cartoon lovers', but complained that Garfield's slow movement and weak moves made the game too frustrating. They concluded, 'Fans of the comic strip might enjoy this platform title. The tedious gameplay and hopeless controls will disgruntle anyone else.' It is ultimately, however, one of the most visually stunning Garfield games, and certainly the one that fans should seek out.

The Garfield Show: Threat of the Space Lasagna

'The Garfield Show: Threat of the Space Lasagna' is a video game based on the series *The Garfield Show*, developed by French studio Eko System. It was the first video game based on the series and was released in summer 2010 for the Nintendo Wii. The game supports the Wii Balance Board and Wii Motion Plus. In December 2011, it was released on Microsoft Windows and Nintendo DS in Russia.

The game revolves around sixteen mini-games, which was perfect for the pick-up-and-play motion controls of the Wii system. In single player, the player is only allowed to play as Garfield, while the opposing team (mice or Space Lasagna) are computers. In multiplayer, the players may choose to either be Garfield or the opposing team. The game also includes a story mode, where the player can unlock all the mini-games and hats, and a mini-game mode, where the player can choose any mini-game they have unlocked. In each game, either Garfield tries to stop the opposing team, or the opposing team tries to keep Garfield from thwarting its plans.

There were many similar games on the Wii, such as 'Wii Sports' or the 'Mario Party' series. The game was critically panned as lacklustre, and its sales were also generally poor, released at a time when the Wii's lifespan was winding down, making way for its successor, the Wii U.

In the game, while Garfield is sleeping, the Space Lasagna are planning their return to Earth to take revenge on Garfield for stopping their scheme in the episode 'Pasta Wars'. They discover that Garfield is friendly with the mice, so decide to take control of them and make the mice wreak havoc around the city while the Space Lasagna go ahead with their plan. Later that day, after the Space Lasagna start their plan, Garfield wakes and finds his mouse friend Squeak hiding. Squeak tells Garfield how the Space Lasagna have exerted mind control over his family, and Garfield decides to save Squeak's family and stop the Space Lasagna from invading the planet.

Garfield: Lasagna World Tour

'Garfield: Lasagna World Tour' is a 2007 budget action-adventure video game developed by EKO Software and published by Blast Entertainment Ltd and Conspiracy Games. It was released for PlayStation 2 and PC and aimed squarely at kids.

In this ten-level action platformer, gamers got the opportunity to take the normally sedentary feline through Mexico, Italy and Egypt on a treasure hunt for his favourite dish. Players can also use Odie in tricky situations, and Garfield can climb on the back of his canine companion for high-speed chase sequences. Garfield can also try on a number of outfits that turn him into a soccer player, cowboy and chef, among others, with each new ensemble giving him special powers.

The Paws TV channel is organizing a treasure hunt known as The Lasagna World Tour. Every day, the winner will receive his or her weight in lasagna for the rest of their lives! Interest thoroughly piqued, Garfield sets out on a tour to find the ultimate in treasure.

The *IGN* review of this game is not particularly kind:

'Everything about "Garfield: Lasagna World Tour" screams cheap. Yeah, it's a budget game ... but that doesn't mean it has to feel like one in almost every respect. That the game was obviously given almost no attention as it was pushed through the approvals process on multiple fronts just underscores how worthless it really was not just to the people making and releasing the game, but to anyone even considering picking it up. Don't do it.'

Garfield Gets Real

'Garfield Gets Real' is an action video game based on the film of the same name. It was developed by Zushi Games in North America and released nearly two years after the original film on 21 July 2009 for the Nintendo DS. Players control Garfield through seven levels of the game. Each level is a mini-game. In levels 1–5, Garfield must collect a certain amount of food. In level 6, bizarrely, Garfield must dance to prove that he is still Garfield, while in level 7 he must rescue Odie.

On *Metacritic*, the game was given an aggregated score of 39/100, based on four critics, indicating generally unfavourable reviews. A *GameZone* review commented, 'Some decent variety in the mechanics and a fairly amusing premise aren't enough to save "Garfield Gets Real" from its monotonous and absurd level design. Very young devotees may find it a briefly amusing adventure, but this really feels more like an advertisement that someone is expecting you to pay money for.'

Cancelled Games

'Garfield' is an unfinished video game prototype that was developed for the Atari 2600. The game was never released due to the video game crash of 1983, a large-scale recession in the video game industry that occurred from 1983–85, primarily in the United States. The crash was attributed to several factors, including market saturation in the number of game consoles and available games, and waning interest in console games in favour of personal computers. Revenues peaked at around $3.2 billion in 1983, then fell to around $100 million by 1985 (a drop of almost 97 per cent). The crash abruptly ended what is retrospectively considered the second generation of console video gaming in North America.

The 'Garfield' game revolves around Garfield trying to find Nermal while running away from Odie. He starts off by hopping around the fence and eating burgers. Next he ducks as flowerpots are thrown at him while he's on the fence. Then he has to cross the top of the roof to get to the other side of the yard, but he must watch out for Odie, who likes to sneak up on him. He has to jump on top of a dog pound of Odies eating burgers, while again avoiding flowerpots. Finally, he has to rescue Nermal, who's hanging on for dear life from the roof. Due to the game being unfinished, it then restarts with the screens in a different order.

The ROM for this game was never allowed to be released or seen until Jim Davis gave its designer permission to distribute it, but it has found a new life on the internet. The box art can be seen on the internet too. On 7 May 2020, musician Nicky Flowers streamed himself on the Twitch live-streaming platform setting a world record high score in the game with 1, 909,896,121,651,051,877,238,357,850 (1.9 octillion). This was allegedly the highest recorded score in any video game in history: a bit strange for a cancelled video game!

Garfield Kart and Garfield Kart: Furious Racing

'Garfield Kart' is a racing video game released on PC in 2013, and in 2015 for the Nintendo 3DS and Steam. It was formerly available on Android and iOS. 'Garfield Kart' takes on the standard template of a kart racing game inspired by the likes of 'Super Mario Kart', 'SEGA All Stars Racing' and 'Crash Team Racing'. An update of 'Garfield Kart', 'Garfield Kart: Furious Racing', was released in 2019. The later game's tracks and cups are the exact same as the original: Lasagna Cup (Catz in the Hood, Crazy Dunes, Palerock Lake, City Slicker); Pizza Cup (Country Bumpkin, Spooky Manor, Mally Market, Valley of the Kings); Burger Cup (Misty for Me, Sneak-a-Peak, Blazing Oasis, Pastacosi Factory); Ice Cream Cup (Mysterious Temple, Prohibited Site, Caskou Park, Loopy Lagoon). 'Garfield Kart: Furious Racing' was released on 6 November 2019 for PC, and 19 November that year for Nintendo Switch, PlayStation 4 and Xbox One, a remake of the original ported to the new generation of video game consoles.

Reviews for both games were quite mixed, but a *Nintendo Life* review was particularly negative:

> 'You're looking for a final insult to round this off, we can feel it. Something to really drive home the point that there's nothing to salvage from this sorry affair. Well, put this in your exhaust pipe: at launch the Switch version is more than double the price of the same game on Steam. Even more bizarrely, there's currently a Steam bundle where you can buy "Furious Racing" and the original "Garfield Kart" – which, remember, is what "Furious Racing" actually is, only more broken – for less than "Furious Racing" alone. As if they are saying: "These games are so bad that the more you want, the less we can morally charge you."'

Chapter 13

Comic Books

In 2012, comic book publishers Boom Studios gained the rights from Paws, Inc. to publish Garfield comics, seeing Garfield transition from a traditional three-panel comic strip to a twenty-two-page comic strip. With the longer format, Boom sought to engage younger comic book readers, as well as delivering consistent longer-form Garfield storytelling. It's strange that a comic book company hadn't tried to publish Garfield comic books before Boom Studios. Boom are most notable for publishing books based on popular licences like *Buffy The Vampire Slayer*, *Firefly* and Jim Henson's *The Storyteller*.

The first volume was officially described as an 'an extra-large collection of the fat cat's return to comics! Garfield and the gang have returned to comics in a big way, and this delicious package brings the fun home to you & your family. Written by GARFIELD & FRIENDS TV Show scribe Mark Evanier, and drawn by the amazing team of Gary Barker, Dan Davis, and Mike DeCarlo, you'll enjoy this as much as Garf loves lasagna!' The Garfield series lasted for thirty-six issues, finishing in April 2015 with a reimagining of *Garfield's 9 Lives*, the television special.

Since then, Boom have been producing one-off comics and original graphic novels for Garfield, the latest of which, *Garzilla*, was released in 2019.

The official blurb for *Garzilla* stated, 'A secret science experiment goes awry, unleashing giant pets – iguanas, ferrets, hamsters and birds – upon an unsuspecting city. Can a super-sized Garfield save the day? The Cat returns in an all-new original graphic novel, featuring an extra large story by Garfield regulars Scott Nickel & Antonio Alfaro about the biggest Garfield ever, as well as a story featuring the return of private eye, Sam Spayed. Also, cartoonist Lee Gatlin joins the party to write & illustrate a short where Jon, in a quest to grow a beard, may have turned into a werewolf!'

Chapter 14

Feature Films

Garfield returned to the headlines in a major way in 2004 with the release of the blockbuster *Garfield: The Movie*, a mix of live action and state-of-the-art computer animation, starring Bill Murray as the voice of Garfield. The film was a rousing box office success, made on a budget of $50 million and earning $200 million. The film also starred Jennifer Love Hewitt as Dr Liz Wilson, Breckin Meyer as Jon Arbuckle, Debra Messing as Arlene and Alan Cumming as Persnikitty. The film was directed by Peter Hewitt, whose previous work includes *Bill & Ted's Bogus Journey* and *The Borrowers*.

Hewitt said of the film:

> 'Actually it was very quick in that it didn't end up in development hell. I was sitting in [Fox Chairman] Tom Rothman's office and he pointed to the volleyball in the corner from *Castaway* and he said that movie took seven years to make. Comparatively speaking we were fast-tracked because I think there was a demand for family-type fare, and we were there at the right time. We worked on the treatment for the movie in May, we made it through the first draft in August, to the fifth draft in November and in February we were in production. The biggest block of time has been animating Garfield. We were done with principal and secondary photography a year ago.'

The film stands out in many ways, including placing Garfield and Jon's home in suburban Detroit, and largely grounds Garfield in the real world.

The plot for the film sees the Garfield we know and love – an overweight, lazy and free-spirited orange cat – living with his owner Jon Arbuckle in a cul-de-sac in Ferndale, a suburb of Detroit, Michigan. Garfield passes his time by antagonizing Jon and teasing his aggressive neighbour, Luca, a Doberman. Aside from Jon, Garfield maintains an unlikely friendship with a helpful mouse, Louis. Garfield also socializes with his fellow neighbourhood cats, including Garfield's stooge Nermal and Arlene.

Meanwhile, a local television host, Happy Chapman, known for his cat Persnikitty, is introduced as a supposedly happy man. In reality he is allergic to cats, jealous of his news reporter brother Walter J. Chapman, and wants to be more successful than him by performing on TV show *Good Day New York*. Jon has made a habit of taking Garfield to the vets, in order to see vet Liz (with whom he is in love). Jon tries to ask Liz out, but due to a misunderstanding, is given custody of a dog named Odie, who is lovable, playful and friendly. Jon and Liz do begin dating. Garfield begins to dislikes Odie and tries to get rid of him. Odie is taken to a canine talent show, where Liz is a judge. Garfield becomes involved in an altercation there with other dogs, and Odie begins dancing to 'Hey Mama' by the Black Eyed Peas.

Odie's improvised performance is a hit. Happy Chapman, who also is a judge of the dog show, is impressed and offers Jon a television deal for Odie, but Jon declines, making Happy more determined than ever to upstage his brother. When Garfield returns home, he hits a ball in frustration, causing a chain reaction that trashes Jon's house. When Jon finds his house in ruins, he makes Garfield sleep outside for the night. Heartbroken, Garfield sadly sings 'New Dog State of Mind'. When Odie comes out to comfort Garfield, he gets back inside and locks Odie out. Nermal and Arlene witness this as Odie runs away, only to be picked up by an elderly woman, Mrs Baker. Jon searches with Liz for Odie while the neighbourhood animals accuse Garfield of locking Odie out and making him run away. Meanwhile, Chapman and his assistant Wendell find a notice Mrs Baker created of Odie and, recognizing the lucrative possibilities, claim Odie as Happy's own, kidnap Odie and give Mrs Baker an autograph.

When Garfield sees Odie on television and hears Chapman announce he and Odie are going to New York City, Garfield sets out to rescue Odie. Jon, discovering Garfield is also missing, asks Liz to start searching for him and Odie. Garfield gets into the broadcast tower via the air vents and finds Odie locked in a kennel, but Chapman enters and secures a shock collar to Odie, which releases an electric discharge that forces Odie to perform tricks.

Chapman heads for the train station with Garfield in close pursuit. However, an animal control officer catches Garfield, mistaking him for a stray. Meanwhile, Mrs Baker tells Jon that Chapman took Odie, making him believe Garfield was taken by him too. Jon and Liz race to the broadcast tower and then to the train station after learning Chapman has left. At the same time, Garfield is released from the pound by Chapman's abandoned feline star Persnikitty, who is really named Sir Roland, along with the other animals. Chapman boards a New York-bound train, with Odie in the luggage car. Garfield sneaks into the train system control room and frantically switches the tracks, leading to an impending train wreck, but hits an emergency control and causes the train to return to the station. Garfield frees Odie and they exit the train. Chapman chases them and corners the two in a luggage area. Chapman threatens Odie with the shock collar, but is stopped by Garfield's friends and animals from the pound, led by Sir Roland. They swarm and attack Chapman, allowing Odie and Garfield to escape.

The collar is now on Chapman, who receives a nasty shock. Jon and Liz arrive to reclaim the animals and find Chapman disoriented. Jon punches Chapman for stealing 'both' his pets – Garfield says that he wasn't stolen and that he was doing the rescue work – and leaves with Liz and the two animals. Chapman is arrested for his supposed involvement with the trains, as well as for abducting Odie, while Garfield regains the respect of his animal friends. Back at home, Liz and Jon form a relationship and Garfield learns a lesson about friendship.

Bill Murray has famously stated that he mistakenly accepted the role, thinking the script was written by Joel Coen (of the famous directing brothers responsible for such films as *No Country For Old Men*, *Fargo* and *The Big Lewbowski*), but it turned out that it was Joel Cohen, who had written films like *Cheaper By The Dozen* and *Money Talks* and had contributed to the *Toy Story* script.

Murray told *GQ* magazine:

'Finally, I went out to LA to record my lines. And usually when you're looping a movie, if it takes two days, that's a lot. I don't know if I should even tell this story, because it's kind of mean. What the hell? It's interesting.

'So I worked all day and kept going, "That's the line? Well, I can't say that." And you sit there and go, "What can I say that will make this funny? And make it make sense?" And I worked. I was exhausted, soaked with sweat, and the lines got worse and worse. And I said, "OK, you better show me the whole rest of the movie, so we can see what we're dealing with."

'So I sat down and watched the whole thing, and I kept saying, "Who the hell cut this thing? Who did this? What the f*** was Coen thinking?" And then they explained it to me: it wasn't written by that Joel Coen.'

Co-writer Alec Sokolow disputed Murray's claim in 2014, stating, 'He knew it was not Joel Coen well before he met Joel Cohen. It's a funny take. And it kind of defends him against the criticism of making such an overtly commercial film. But, it's complete horse shit.'

Murray's experiences and perceptions of the film sum up the general critical response, which was mostly negative. Many critics pointed towards a poor script, uninteresting story and bland romance in the film, but there were some positives, with some critics noting that Murray's performance was perfect for the lazy feline. A.O. Scott of *The New York Times* wrote: 'That Garfield speaks in the supercilious, world-weary drawl of Bill Murray is some small consolation, as are a few of the animal tricks.' Legendary film critic Roger Ebert wrote a favourable review, giving it three out of four stars as he commented, 'Although Garfield claims "I don't do chases", the movie does have a big chase scene and other standard plot ingredients, but it understands that Garfield's personality, his behavior, his glorious self-absorption, are what we're really interested in. The Davis strip is not about a story but about an attitude.'

Picking up on Murray's trashing of the film, in the movie *Zombieland*, he plays himself as a survivor of a zombie apocalypse. When he is shot by one of the group of survivors, he is asked if he has any regrets; he replies, 'Garfield, maybe.'

Davis, on the other hand, was ecstatic about the casting of Murray as his creation:

'It was because of Bill Murray's attitude [that he was cast]. It wasn't really so much his voice. It was the fact that he embodies the attitude that Garfield has always displayed in the strip. Lorenzo [Music] obviously wasn't a choice since he passed away years ago, and when the producers said, "Bill Murray would like to do the voice," I thought, "Oh, cool." My biggest concern about doing a CGI Garfield with live action was that people wouldn't buy into the fact that this was *our* Garfield – the Garfield we'd known all these years. But I thought that as soon as they heard Bill Murray's voice they'd get it. There will be that emotional tag going with his voice. That will establish the fact that, "Yes, this character has attitude."

'The producers of the movies wanted a name actor to do Garfield's voice in order to bolster the draw. Since we held out no hope of casting a Lorenzo Music sound-alike, we sought an actor with Garfield's attitude. Only two came to mind: Bill Murray and Jack Nicholson. We never got to Jack.'

While John Goodman was also rumoured to be in mind for the role, the producers would end up with Bill Murray for better or for worse.

Despite all the criticisms and Murray's tongue-in-cheek negativity, a sequel was produced by the same team and *Garfield: A Tale Of Two Kitties* was released in 2006. The sequel featured the majority of the voice cast from the first film, with the addition of Tim Curry, Bob Hoskins, Richard E. Grant, Vinny Jones, Joe Pasquale and Rhys Ifans as computer-generated animal counterparts for Garfield to interact with. The cast also included Billy Connolly, Roger Rees and Ian Abercrombie as live-action actors. The film had a budget of $60 million dollars and almost tripled its budget in takings. Both films are seen as commercial successes, but critical failures. *A Tales Of Two Kitties*, which was based on Mark Twain's novel *The Prince and the Pauper*, was nominated for two Golden Raspberry awards in 2006, in the categories 'Worst Prequel or Sequel' and 'Worst Excuse for Family Entertainment', but lost out to *Basic Instinct 2* and *RV*, respectively.

The plot for the sequel has Jon Arbuckle planning to propose to vet Dr Liz, who is going on a business trip to London. Jon follows her to the UK as a surprise, and after escaping from the kennels, Garfield and Odie sneak into Jon's luggage and join him on the trip. A bored Garfield and Odie break out of Jon's hotel room, and subsequently become lost in the streets of London.

Meanwhile, at Carlyle Castle in the English countryside, the late Lady Eleanor Carlyle's will is read. She bequeaths the castle to Prince XII, her beloved cat, a Garfield look-alike. This enrages Lady Carlyle's nephew, Lord Manfred Dargis, who will only receive a stipend of £50 a week and inherit the grand estate once Prince passes away. Lord Dargis subsequently traps Prince in a picnic basket and throws him into the river.

Garfield inadvertently switches places with Prince after Jon finds Prince climbing out of a drain, and Jon later takes Prince to the hotel, mistaking him for Garfield, while Prince's butler Smithee finds Garfield in the street and takes him to Carlyle Castle, believing him to be Prince.

In the grand estate Garfield is residing in, he receives a great deal of special treatment, including a butler and a group of four-legged servants and followers. Garfield teaches his new animal friends how to make lasagne, while Prince learns to adapt to his new life with Jon. Dargis sees Garfield and thinks Prince has come back – if the lawyers see Prince/Garfield, they will not sign the estate over to Dargis, who secretly wants to destroy the castle and barnyard and kill the animals to build a spa resort. Dargis makes many attempts to kill Garfield, one involving a merciless yet dim-witted Rottweiler named Rommel.

Eventually, Garfield and Prince meet each other for the first time and they convince the other animals to help them defeat Dargis' dastardly scheme. Jon and Odie discover the mix-up and go to the castle, which Liz is coincidentally visiting.

Garfield and Prince taunt Dargis, whose plan is exposed, and they are seen by the lawyers handling the disposal of the estate. Dargis barges in, holding a blunderbuss and threatening everybody if they don't sign the papers giving him ownership of the estate, and takes Liz hostage. Jon attempts to force Dargis to release Liz by holding a crossbow at him, only for Dargis to threaten to kill Jon for getting involved. Garfield and Prince, with the help of Odie and Jon, save the day; Smithee alerts the authorities and Dargis is arrested for his crimes. Garfield, who had been trying to stop Jon from proposing to Liz, has a change of heart. He helps Jon propose, and she accepts.

Roger Ebert famously wrote a review of the film from the perspective of Garfield, featuring lots of cat-based humour and puns.

Singer Prince was originally chosen for the role of Prince XII, but he opted out at the last minute, so the producers had to scrap all the relevant animation and start over with Tim Curry, their second choice.

As well as the live action/CGI films, Garfield also featured in several DVD films in the early 2000s, including *Garfield Gets Real*, *Garfield's Fun Fest* and *Garfield's Pet Force*. Renowned voice actor Frank Welker – known for his roles in *Futurama*, *Transformers* and *Scooby Doo* – took on the role of Garfield for the three films, giving a voice that is completely different to those done by Lorenzo Music and Bill Murray.

Garfield Gets Real

Garfield Gets Real is a CGI film that was released in theatres on 9 August 2007 and on DVD on 20 November that year. It was produced by Paws, Inc., in cooperation with Davis Entertainment, and would spawn two sequels, *Garfield's Fun Fest* and *Garfield's Pet Force*.

The film follows Garfield's life as a comic strip celebrity and his desire to live a normal life in the real world. Garfield lives with Odie and Jon in a suburban town inhabited by cartoon characters within the Comic Strip World. Garfield and the gang work at Comic Studios with other comic characters. The comic strip is made in Comic Strip World and sent to 'The Real World', where it is put in the newspaper. But Garfield is tired of the same old jokes his friends crack and bored with his work and life in Comic Strip World, longing to go to The Real World.

Odie, unwilling to return a prop bone, tries to hide it and ends up opening a patch in the screen. The danger alarm is rung, and everyone panics. Eli, the Head Technician of Comic Studios, explains to the comic characters that the screen separates Comic Strip World from The Real World, with no way back. Garfield sees his chance to go to The Real World (and eat hot dogs) and goes through the screen without anyone noticing. When the comic characters realize Garfield is in The Real World, Eli blocks the patch in the screen by using special tape. Odie also winds up in The Real World, gets his bone back, and he and Garfield go to find some dinner. Garfield meets a cat named Shecky, who invites Garfield and Odie to dinner and a show. As they chat, Odie is chased by a gang of chihuahuas who want his bone. Garfield goes to save Odie and eventually defeats the chihuahuas. Shecky and the duo head to a fence (which is known as Club Shecky) where the dinner and show are, and meet two other pets, Waldo and Sheila. Shecky gets dinner by performing a 'show' for the people who live in a nearby building. The residents, who are trying to sleep, are annoyed and start throwing leftover food at him. After dinner, Shecky brings Garfield and Odie to their new home, an abandoned hotel called Hotel Muncie.

The next day, Garfield finds a newspaper in the trash and learns his strip will be cancelled. He sees an article asking people to audition and replace Garfield. Garfield and Odie head for the place where they are doing try-outs. The judges are not impressed by the others auditioning, and Garfield and Odie also fail. The judges are more impressed in Hale and Hardy, a muscular dog and cat. One of the judges, Sid, decides to give Garfield one more chance: if Garfield's strip isn't back in the paper in twenty-four hours, he and the judges will have to deal with Hale and Hardy. Garfield has an idea of building a bigger version of a concertina tunnel that Wally, another comic strip character, had invented that can go through the screen back to Comic Studios, and shares the idea with his friends back in Comic Strip World. Wally and the other comic strip characters start building the giant concertina.

Later that night, Garfield and Odie return to Hotel Muncie. Hale and Hardy sneak into the hotel, go into Garfield, Odie and Shecky's room and tie them up, taunting them before leaving. As they close the door, a candle is knocked over and sets fire to a newspaper, causing the entire hotel to catch fire. Eli finds out about this and calls everyone to the screen. Wally and the others complete the finishing touches to the giant concertina tunnel, and Wally asks for two volunteers to help him save Garfield, Odie and Shecky. Billy Bear – another comic strip character, who shares a strip with Randy Rabbit – and Jon volunteer to go with Wally to save the three friends, and go through the screen by going into the giant concertina tunnel. They enter the burning hotel through a small hole in the wall, free the three friends and prepare to escape, but the entire hotel is in flames and the ceiling begins to collapse, blocking the exits. Luckily, Shecky finds a trash cart that they can ride in. Jon, Wally, Odie, Garfield and Shecky jump in. Billy Bear pushes the cart and jumps in too, and they go down the staircase. Garfield winds up on the chandelier with Odie; the chandelier collapses, causing the cart and chandelier to fall to the ground. The cart crashes out of the hotel and flings all six of them into the concertina, the door of the tunnel closes and disappears and they are transported back to Comic Strip World.

Some days later, Hale and Hardy, now out of jobs, are shown reading the newspaper stating that Garfield and Odie are back in the comic strips. They blame each other for this. Waldo and Sheila are on their own now that Shecky is in the comic strips. The comic characters dance and celebrate the return of Garfield. Unknown to the comic characters, the chihuahuas have also gone through the concertina tunnel, and the film ends with them chasing Odie.

This was the first Garfield film to be written by Jim Davis himself since *Garfield Gets a Life* in 1991.

In Garfield's bedroom, a panel from the 8 June 2003 comic strip, with Garfield up against a dog's posterior, is seen framed on the wall.

Starting with this movie, Frank Welker, Wally Wingert, Jason Marsden and Audrey Wasilewski become the official voices for Garfield, Jon, Nermal and Arlene, respectively. Gregg Berger reprised his role as Odie.

Garfield's Fun Fest

This was released on 5 August 2008, and, like the previous film, was written by Jim Davis.

In the film, Garfield is reminded several times that the thirtieth annual Fun Fest is coming up. Garfield has won the previous twenty-nine Fun Fests. However, Arlene is tired of the same old routine she is always in with Garfield; this time, she wants tango-dancing. Later, a mysterious stranger named Ramone is introduced, a cheesy-accent Mexican cat. After Garfield leaves Arlene, he realizes that he has lost all his hope and fears he has no humour left. With Odie and the help of a storybook (later revealed to be a fictional story), they travel to the Mysterious Forest of Humour to drink the legendary funny water, which was the inspiration of the creator of humour technology, Freddy Frog. Freddy explains to Garfield that funny water does not exist, that he just had to believe in himself, and there was no need to come to the forest with Odie. Taking a wooden airplane to fly back to the Comic Studios, they crash-land and see Ramone hosting as the MC, having made Arlene suffer a nauseous dizzy-spin in the tango. Garfield puts himself forward and dons a Mexican tango costume to battle Ramone. Ramone and Garfield face each other in the Fun Fest, where Ramone is revealed as a cyborg.

Garfield turns the tables on the cyborg impostor by pulling his head off, and it is revealed that it was Nermal controlling Ramone all along. Nermal is disqualified and Garfield is named the winner, continuing his dancing of the tango with Arlene and the legend of his success in his own life and Cartoon World. Nermal tries to come up with another plan to win next year's Fun Fest, but Odie is sceptical of his ideas. Garfield and Arlene kiss, and the film ends with Freddy flying his wooden airplane over the Comic Studios.

Garfield's Pet Force

The final direct-to-video film has Professor Wally on the planet Dorkon showing Emperor Jon his new invention, the Molecular Scrambler (MoScram) ray gun, a device powered by the Klopman crystal that can scramble inanimate objects and organisms into new creatures. Emperor Jon is more concerned about finding a wife to continue the royal bloodline. When a warship lands near the palace, Emperor Jon sees Vetvix (the super-villain counterpart to Dr Liz Wilson) and asks to marry her. She agrees, but before Jon can kiss Vetvix, she steals the MoScram gun and zombifies Jon's guards. Professor Wally calls the Pet Force: Garzooka (Garfield's superhero counterpart), Odious (Odie), Abnermal (Nermal) and Starlena (Arlene).

The situation is then revealed to be just a Pet Force comic book that Nermal was reading. Nermal is really excited about getting the 100th edition issue. Garfield's friends go to the Comic Studio to work on their new strip, but Garfield wants to finish all the hot dogs. Nermal gets the new Pet Force issue from a newsstand, but Garzooka jumps out of one of the comic books. Garzooka heads for Jon's house and is told where Odie, Arlene and Nermal are by Garfield. Garzooka gives Garfield the Klopman Crystal, telling him to protect it. Curiously, the pages of the comic book show exactly what is going on in Comic Strip World with Garfield and his group, but pages of future incidents are blank until they occur.

In the break room at the Comic Studio, Nermal, Arlene and Odie notice Garzooka behind them. Garzooka hands them special serums and asks them to help him stop Vetvix, but they don't change immediately after drinking the serums. It's now time for Odie, Arlene and Nermal to return to work, and Garzooka follows them. Meanwhile, the real Garfield is enjoying a relaxing day by himself but is captured by Vetvix, who tortures him for the Klopman Crystal, but to no avail. Garfield tries to protect the Klopman Crystal, but it is taken by Vetvix, who orders her guards to get rid of Garfield.

Garzooka and the Pet Force go to the antenna and use it to bring down Vetvix's ship. Meanwhile, zombies chase Garfield and Wally to the Comic Studio, and Eli opens the pit in the filming area, into which the zombies fall. Meanwhile, at the tower, Vetvix shoots the MoScram ray gun at the Pet Force, using the Super Scramble mode.

Emperor Jon and Professor Wally break free, using the Professor's monocle that Garfield put on the windowsill earlier, and take over the ship, flying away and making Vetvix fall off. However, she makes a giant monster by shooting the ray gun at most of the buildings in the Comic Strip World, and decides to use the monster to destroy everything and get back her ship. Meanwhile, Vetvix's ship lands near the back alley of Comic Studio, and the crew meet Professor Wally and Emperor Jon, who let Garfield enter the ship. The ship flies above the monster and Garfield jumps off. By using the power of the Super Scrambled Pet Force and the dropped MoScram ray gun, Garfield defeats the monster and unscrambles the Pet Force.

Garfield goes inside Comic Studio, and he and the crew surround Vetvix; she backs herself into a corner called the 'Smile Section'. Garfield shoots Vetvix with the ray gun, turning Vetvix into a nice woman, and she says sorry to Jon and kisses him. Eli opens the pit and Garfield unscrambles the zombies. Garzooka gives the red serums to Odie, Arlene and Nermal, and they drink it, while Garfield gives the MoScram ray gun back to Professor Wally, who intends to destroy it after restoring Dorkon. The Comic Studio employees, the Pet Force, Garfield and his friends watch Vetvix and Emperor Jon's wedding.

Garfield sits outside, thinking about how much he missed out on life, and he and Arlene dance into the sky before returning to Earth. The Comic Studio employees watch the wedding of Jon and Vetvix. They later find that Comic Studio director Charles' assistant Betty has followed Garzooka back to Dorkon, much to Garzooka's annoyance and Charles' shock. Arlene tells him he might need a new assistant, which Nermal (now in costume) decides to apply for.

At the time of writing, Alcon Films was planning to release fully CGI Garfield films, but as of then nothing had emerged.

Garfield Apps

Of course, with the invention of the internet and mobile phones it was only a matter of time before Garfield would become the face of a mobile app.

The Garfield brand was added to Rooplay in June 2017. Rooplay offers over 500 games for children aged 2–8 in a single app, with no downloads. Each game is claimed to have been meticulously checked to ensure they are child-safe and fun to play. You can teach your child to spell with Garfield's ABC's or develop their early maths skills with Garfield's Math Bingo.

There are now many Garfield apps – too many to list them all – but most are either a standard variation on a popular game, like a Garfield version of Candy Crush, or educational apps for younger children

The Garfield Trail and Heritage Museum

The town of Fairmount boasts a couple of famous Indiana natives. In addition to its most well-known son, movie star James Dean, Fairmount is also the hometown of Jim Davis, creator of Garfield. Jim Davis' Paws, Inc. studio is just a short drive from Fairmount. Davis and Garfield's presence continue to be felt throughout Indiana with Grant County's Garfield Trail, where you can visit fourteen unique statues of America's favourite lasagne-loving fat cat. Located in Marion and surrounding Grant County cities, the fibreglass statues are each approximately 5ft high and depict Garfield in captivating costumes or funny situations. Taking a trip along the Garfield Trail is said to be a great family activity and presents a number of fun photo opportunities.

Chapter 15

The Internet, Memes and Beyond

Garfield is perfect for the internet generation, with his collection of catchphrases such as 'I hate Mondays'. Garfield Minus Garfield is a website devised to show just what the title says, what happens in the Garfield comic when it has no Garfield. Garfield Minus Garfield was created by Dubliner Dan Walsh and was originally made as a Tumblr site. It turns into Jon talking to himself, looking like an existential crisis on the three panels with a big gap missing where Garfield should be. There is a particularly poignant strip which features Jon saying, 'Do you ever get the feeling no one cares about you?' in the first panel, then in the second panel he stands there blankly and in the third there is just nothing. Taking Garfield away actually gives the comic strip a second meaning, turning it into a poignant rumination on what it means to be human.

Walsh says, 'Sometimes the world can feel like a pretty intimidating place, and it takes someone like Jon to remind you to lighten up and laugh at the hopelessness of it all.'

One of Walsh's occasional readers is Davis himself, who was intrigued when he heard about the site. The cartoonist called the work 'an inspired thing to do' and thanked Walsh for enabling him to see another side of Garfield.

'Believe it or not, I am a fan of Garfield,' Walsh has stated, as many believe that his site was created to look upon the character negatively. 'I do find the original strip funny, but not as funny as Garfield Minus Garfield (because that's my taste). It's a completely different comic once Garfield has been removed. It suddenly becomes more surreal and dark, more *Monty Python* than Dick Van Dyke, more *South Park* than *The Simpsons*.'

Davis has said, 'It was kind of funny – we called Dan, and the second we identified ourselves, he said, "I'm so sorry. You want me to cease and desist, right?" We said, "No, we want to collaborate on a book with you."'

Bloggers like Walsh 'see the futility in making everything turn out right every day', Davis says. But, he adds, a little darkness 'makes the positives even sweeter'. It would have been easy for Davis and Paws, Inc. to try to shut down this internet creation, but Davis sees the joy within it and that it embraces the culture around his creation, even encouraging it somewhat.

Other similar sites include Silent Garfield, where the strips are redone without Garfield's thought balloons, again making Jon the fool who is talking away to his mute cat. In a similar vein, Mason Williams of Tailsteak, the creator of the website Arbuckle by ..., says, 'Garfield changes from being a comic about a sassy, corpulent feline, and becomes a compelling picture of a lonely, pathetic, delusional man who talks to his pets. Consider that Jon, according to Garfield canon, cannot hear his cat's thoughts. This is the world as he sees it. This is his story.'

Davis, too, has seen a darker side of Garfield, but opts not to explore it:

'He takes great delight, yeah, in a lot of other people's pain. He's a bit of a sociopath in that respect. Interesting thought, I never really thought about that, because I personally laugh about everything, but that's not what I put in the strip. It's the edgier, the funnier me, but the trick is to make everyone laugh. One day I want to write the gag that makes the whole world laugh, I think that'd be cool.

'It's more important to have a body of work resonate with the reader than it is to have an individual gag [resonate].'

It is interesting to see that Davis is well aware of certain elements of his creation that permeate in fandom, perhaps even beyond his own interests.

Davis continues, 'He [Garfield] just randomly kicked Odie off the table and he said, "I'm not known for my compassion." So I guess he's not compassionate, which opens him up to a little ... yeah, he's certainly got a dark side.'

Lasagna Cat

Lasagna Cat is a series of YouTube videos created by Fatal Farm. All of them follow the same formula, re-enacting a Garfield comic strip as a live action video, then showing a bizarre music video or 'tribute to Jim Davis', usually relevant to the preceding strip, which often ends with the camera focusing on a mugshot of a smiling Davis. It is a very bizarre series, used as a pastiche of the Garfield strips to show how absurd they actually are.

Garfield is also an inspiration to a generation of teenagers and twenty-somethings who watch random cat videos and other animal videos. There are dedicated accounts to animals doing funny stuff, or animals talking to their owners with subtitles. Garfield was the precursor to famous Instagram animals like Grumpy Cat. All the Instagram animals are just doing what Garfield did years ago. The producers of *Grumpy Cat The Movie* even asked Davis if Garfield could cameo in the film, but Davis turned it down due to other commitments.

In 2017, Garfield was the subject of a war on Wikipedia over his gender. When Davis made the following remark in 2014, it was in an interview with online magazine *Mental Floss*. At first it didn't cause a fuss because no one really paid any attention to it. Davis said in the interview, 'Garfield is very universal. By virtue of being a cat, really, he's not really male or female or any particular race or nationality, young or old.'

These comments would start a heated internet debate regarding the gender of Garfield. On 23 February 2017, user Virgil Texas tweeted a message declaring that Garfield is gender-neutral, citing Davis' description of his character from the Mental Floss article. Shortly after, Texas tweeted a screenshot of Garfield's Wikipedia page which he had edited and updated to list its gender as 'none'. Within a week, Texas' tweets garnered more than 1,800 retweets and 5,800 likes.

Over the next 72 hours, the tweets by Texas set off an edit war on Garfield's Wikipedia page among fans of the cartoon series and supporters of the genderless canon. This led to a lengthy and heated debate over the character's gender identity, with some participants citing original cartoon strips to make their case for and against the gender-neutral identity of Garfield.

By 27 February, the Wikipedia page had been temporarily placed on lock due to 'edit warring/content dispute', though the debate quickly continued after the lock expired in the coming days. Between 24 February and 3 March 2017, more than forty edits were logged by various contributors on the site.

Throughout the week, the online debate on Garfield's gender was picked up by the *Washington Post, Huffington Post, Mashable, New York*

Magazine and *AV Club*, among many others. On 1 March, Twitter user @congressedits tweeted that the Garfield Wikipedia article had been edited anonymously by someone from the US House of Representatives, which garnered more than 1,000 retweets and 1,500 likes.

Davis joined in the debate. 'Garfield is male,' he confirmed to the *Washington Post*, after having to release a statement himself. 'He has a girlfriend, Arlene.'

The cartoonist added, 'I've always said that I wanted to work with animals because they're not perceived as being any particular gender, race, age or ethnicity. In that sense, the humour could be enjoyed by a broader demographic.' Unfortunately, the situation spiralled out of control, but on Wikipedia at the time of publication, Garfield is listed as a male with a reference number beside it, linking to a *Washington Post* article about the controversy.

Davis continued:

'The internet has affected the biggest change in the comics since the very inception of the comic strip. Thirty years ago there were around 300 syndicated cartoonists. There are only so many newspapers and only so much space on the comic's page. Today, anyone can draw a comic strip, put it online, and be a cartoonist. So the ranks of cartoonists have swelled from 300 to, probably, 30 million! And, as cable TV heralded the end of heavily censored programming content, the internet has freed cartoonists to address edgier and more mature subject matter.

'The fact of the matter is that a lot of these young cartoonists are very good, and that's a motivator for our generation of cartoonists.'

Garfield Gameboy'd

Garfield Gameboy'd is a series of short videos by Lumpy Touch. They are about an alternate reality where Garfield is a Lovecraftian monster trying to hunt his owner, Jon Arbuckle.

Lumpy Touch, also known as plain Lumpy, is a pixel art animator and Twitch streamer, first recognized for the *Garfield Gameboy'd* series. Before he started animating on YouTube, Lumpy used to mainly draw pictures for his DeviantArt, Pixel Joint and Tumblr account. In October

2018, he released *Garfield Gameboy'd Part 1* as his first animation, which gained notability around the internet. Since then, he has made many more animations that are usually peculiar or unnerving, with the occasional wholesome animation.

Go to http://garfieldminusgarfield.tumblr.com for further information.

Criticism

In a *New York Times* article by Brian Feldman published in January 2016, headlined 'Hating Garfield Is the Web's Oldest Sport', the writer says, 'People *hate* Garfield. Performative hatred of Garfield is a pervasive subculture online and has been for many years.' Certainly, there are many criticisms that are levelled at the cartoon cat. In terms of online content, Twitter users often direct hatred at Garfield under posts about Monday, while Tumblr sites like IHateJonArbuckle continue to gain in popularity. Articles such as those published by *Slate* entitled 'Is Garfield Supposed to be Funny' continue to trickle out over the years. Even back in 2007, there were sites pre-Garfield Minus Garfield removing the thought bubbles in the books to show the absurdity of the characters.

It's hard to tell where the hatred comes from. Certainly, the endless merchandising is a reason for some people, along with the commercialism and capitalism that the brand represents. Perhaps they see the character as something of a sell-out, a cynical character devised to sell plush toys, for his face to be adorned on toothbrushes, toilet seats (yes, toilet seats), umbrellas, credit cards and everything else. There is a legitimacy that people tend to forego when Garfield is mentioned, feeling that it is an empty brand and that Davis is a crass ad man devoted to making millions of dollars, pestering food stores to get advertising deals for Garfield. It isn't viewed in the same way as Calvin and Hobbes or Peanuts, despite Peanuts certainly having a similar amount of marketing power behind it. Interviewers focus on the fact that in the 1980s, Davis claimed he'd work on the strips for fifteen hours a week, while he worked more than triple that for the advertising and licencing department. It's an attempt to delegitimize the creation because of the commercial aspect.

The *Slate* article argues:

'The strip serves to keep Garfield in the public eye as a creative character, but the public eye isn't really on print newspapers that much anymore, and the daily newspaper comics section is probably one of the most moribund elements of popular culture in existence today. Good for Davis in maximizing the potential of his creation, but as a humor, it has dubious roots. Peanuts and The Family Circle were actually funny, once upon a time. Garfield, not so much.'

In the end, Garfield does not have the profound nature of strips like Calvin and Hobbes, nor does it have the reflections on childhood of Peanuts, but it never sought either of those things. Davis simply sought to give people a laugh during a bad day, and he shouldn't be criticised for that. It's similar to Swedish music journalists always sniping at Abba. Before Abba, Swedish music was largely folk protest music, but when Abba came along, they changed everything. Journalists didn't like them because they wanted breezy fun, so ultimately their legacy of saccharine pop is viewed differently. However, there is nothing wrong with the escapism and fun they presented; sometimes that's what people want. That is what Garfield the cat represents to people, a small bit of escapism during your day. Calvin and Hobbes is a sometimes funny, sometimes painful look at childhood; it is engaging, while Garfield is not, and ultimately there isn't anything wrong with that.

For many creators, the path of Jim Davis is an inspiring one. From small-town beginnings to a global empire, his journey represents one unlike any other. Garfield represents one of the most successful franchises in pop culture, having been built from the ground up by Davis, who retained everything from marketing to creative control and foreign rights. Whereas many creators give up a lot when they create something, sacrificing action figure rights or giving up creative control in film, Davis did not do any of that. He stayed true to his vision.

Bill Watterson, creator of Calvin and Hobbes, has been famously critical of both Garfield and U.S. Acres. In an interview, he said Garfield was 'consistent' and that 'Jim Davis has his factory in Indiana cranking out this strip about a pig on a farm. I find it an insult to the intelligence, though it's very successful.'

Davis responded:

'I want him to be the cat next door and I feel a real responsibility to balance the scales. With what's going on in the economy, in politics, it's awful and very depressing, so the purpose of the comics is to lighten things up.

'We accepted the royalty checks, but my biggest fear was overexposure. We pulled all plush dolls off the shelves for five years.'

Chapter 16

Sale To Viacom

In 2019, Viacom International, parent company of Nickelodeon, acquired the rights to Garfield with the purchase of Paws, Inc. 'Great content is core to the strength of our brands, and Garfield is a beloved character that continues to be part of the cultural zeitgeist with universal resonance across all ages,' said Viacom Media Networks COO Sarah Levy. 'The acquisition of Paws, Inc. provides another opportunity for Viacom to leverage our platforms to extend the global reach of iconic IP.' The sale to Viacom puts Garfield in the same place as brands like Spongebob Squarepants, Teenage Mutant Ninja Turtles, Dora The Explorer and other legacy brands that Nickelodeon have acquired.

Along with the TV series at Nickelodeon, Viacom Nickelodeon Consumer Products manages global merchandising, including existing licensees, while Davis continues drawing the Garfield comic strip that he created back in 1978, which remains the most widely syndicated comic strip in the world.

Davis said of the sale to Nickelodeon, 'I've always tried to make people laugh with humour that is classic and appealing to both kids and adults. I'm delighted that Garfield is going to be placed in the capable hands of the folks at Nick. They know how to entertain and will be great stewards for the franchise. I am also excited to continue to do the thing that gets me out of bed every morning – the comic strip.'

Pam Kaufman, Nickolodeon president, commented, 'Garfield is a global evergreen franchise that is a natural fit with Nickelodeon and our portfolio of iconic properties. With fans around the globe that span both kids and adults, we are excited to ignite Garfield into a multi-generational consumer products juggernaut.'

It means that Davis still has control and creative input, but for the first time in forty years, Garfield is maybe just in the hands of someone else. Davis ensures that Garfield will live on forever, even if Davis does not.

Conclusion

Davis says, 'I look at Peanuts, started in 1950. Blondie, 1929. It gives me a great feeling. I would like for somebody to pick this feature up and continue doing it because it makes people laugh. I would like for it to carry on, because everyone likes to think they had a reason to be.'

Davis is excited for the future of the strip and is empowering tomorrow's cartoonists. Garfield.com is a powerful place where children can learn more about the history of Garfield, engage in mini-games or even make their own strip.

Davis says:

'We actually have software for kids, on our website, which allows them to create comic strips by simply picking shapes, eyes, ears, you know, all the stuff for the avatars. They can create their own without having to draw it out, at least the way we're doing it. It's still preserving the art because cartooning, and the comic strip, is a uniquely American art form. We created it, with *The Yellow Kid*, and then the *Katzenjammer Kids*, so that's something that needs to be preserved.

'I think part of the appeal is, you know, like with *Peanuts*, you always want to go back to see Snoopy on the doghouse. In such a changing world, [readers] want to know that some things stay the same, so I feel a responsibility to keep Garfield loving lasagna and hating Mondays; he's never going to go on a diet.'

It's clear that Davis understands some of the criticisms levelled against his creation. Perhaps it isn't the most inventive strip, nor is it the most heartfelt or even the smartest. However, what Garfield does is make you laugh. It gives the reader a brief moment to escape and enjoy the sarcastic humour of an animal.

David admits,

'It actually just gets easier. It gets easier and easier as you get to know your characters better. And the times change enough that you [always] have a ton of stuff to write about. If anything, writing [Garfield] is easier today than it was thirty years ago. The thing is to relax and have fun with it. I have fun writing stuff that people have fun reading, because you really cannot fool the reader – you have to be laughing yourself.'

Garfield does not have a job, Garfield does not go to school and every day is the same. Nevertheless, every Monday is just a reminder that his life is the same old, same old, cycling again and for some reason even though his life is pretty much the same every day, on Mondays specifically, awful things tend to happen to him physically. Garfield becomes like a feline everyman, ready to say the things we don't want to tell ourselves. Garfield is an escape for many people, and Davis has said that fan response has always been very special to him, knowing that some people have found the silliness of Garfield in dark times:

'There was a teen study and the biggest appeal to teens for Garfield [was] – he makes them laugh, one, and two, he's hip. It totally caught me off guard. There's nothing hip in his dialogue, because nothing will date you any quicker than if you use "tubular". So I avoid that, because people will be eating and sleeping a few generations from now. I guess it's his attitude, so it's not the way he says it, but what he feels. He resents authority and that's always going to be in. He doesn't obey Jon, who is the parental figure. He's hip in that respect, so that's cool.'

In terms of Garfield's longevity, in the 21st Century Comics Poll – a major survey taken by the National Cartoonists Society, with newspaper editors finding out what attracted people to the comics – one of the things they liked was the fact that there was something they could count on. They expected to see Snoopy on his doghouse and they expected to see Garfield go for lasagne.

Davis says:

'In these days when there's so much uncertainty, it's nice to go to a place where you can go back. And I think that's why it was such a shock when Sparky [Charles Schulz, creator of Peanuts] passed away. He'd been doing it for fifty years, he was supposed to do it for another fifty years. For me, it was terrible, it was just crushing. Fifty years! That's not like a sitcom that goes two seasons, or has a great run of eight years, it's like fifty years, that's your life. You grow up, you learn to read, you get married, you raise kids, reading the same comic, you know, with Snoopy laying on the doghouse.'

It speaks to the longevity of Garfield that Davis set out to create a character that was timeless. Garfield may go through small changes, but his appeal is simple and that just about trumps any need for complexity. Much like lasagne is comfort food for many people, reading Garfield or even seeing his familiar face feels comfortable too.

'After I've passed on, I won't care whether he goes on or not, but I've always maintained that when I'm ready to retire, hopefully I'd know when that time comes around,' Davis says. 'If somebody's funny; if someone is really writing well and could keep him going and keep him entertaining, more power to him because that's why Garfield is there.'

With the sale of Garfield to Nickelodeon, it seems that Davis is content with Garfield being in the right hands to carry the feline forward into the next forty years. Davis himself seems to be the reverse of Garfield, meeting the future with relentless optimism. He remains, for now, entrenched in his work, curating Garfield and his pals, finding new adventures, avenues and of course new merchandise. He says he loves Mondays, seeing it as the start of a new week to get it right: 'My dream in life is to write the one gag that makes everyone in the world laugh. So, every week might be the week I get that done.'

There is an earnestness to Davis that he shares with his most famous creation. 'The novelty's not worn off because I'm still trying to get it right.'

Davis said in an interview with the *Guardian*, 'I would like to do it for as long as I feel I have something to contribute to it, until someone taps me on the shoulder and says "Jim, you're not funny anymore, stop it." I can't believe forty years has gone by. It's been like a finger snap.'

While Garfield may not be revered in literary circles, and might not have the same poignancy in the comic strip as a Peanuts or Calvin and Hobbes, it does have staying power and recognizability. Davis and Paws, Inc. use Garfield for environmental and charitable concerns. While Davis started Paws, Inc. with only a few employees, he has grown the company to over forty staff, and that is no mean feat.

That is what many people love about Garfield; even if Davis is not around, it seems that Garfield always will be. Davis' creation no longer belongs to Jim Davis himself, but it belongs to everyone: everyone who has heard 'I hate Mondays', everyone who looks at lasagne and thinks about Garfield, everyone who has been touched in some way by Garfield.